Child-
hood

Child-hood

an anthology
for grown-ups

hood

Compiled by Dewi Roberts

seren

Seren is the book imprint of
Poetry Wales Press Ltd
Nolton Street, Bridgend, Wales
www.seren-books.com

Introduction & Editorial © Dewi Roberts, 2005
Foreword © Stevie Davies, 2005

ISBN 1-85411-378-X
A CIP record for this title is available from
the British Library.

The publisher works with the financial assistance
of the Welsh Books Council.

Cover photograph: Lucy Llewellyn
www.luleephoto.co.uk

Printed in Plantin by Gomer Press, Llandysul

CONTENTS

Part Three: *Yew're the bloody teacher!*

Part Four: *A windy boy and a bit*

Part Five: *Able to hear the sound of the bell*

Coda

Foreword

We are all dead children, haunted by revenants who tender in dream or reverie intimations of our early selves when we were new to the world. The children of Dewi Roberts' choice anthology bring with them the landscape of Wales in many moods and shapes. Not all of us 'Shin'd' in our 'Angell-infancy', as did the seventeenth-century Henry Vaughan amongst the hills and lakes of Brecon. Some were scamps and scapegraces, rushing hither and thither in games innocent of their own transience. All were destined to undergo baptism by water, fire or perplexity, under the institutions of Wales or imposed on Wales – chapel, school, synagogue. Before long, the youngsters are trapped in the guilts of the tribe – like the children who rush away 'through trees from God' in his voice of thunder and lightning in T.H. Jones' 'A Storm in Childhood'. For some Welsh children, like Lorna Sage, the little person entered into a world of emotional stint and crookedness: a gran who liked to pinch, grandfather in his 'rusty cassock', a state of yellow-underweared 'household craziness' and squalor, which the child must accept and somehow adapt to as a norm.

Each of the passages of prose and poetry chosen by Dewi Roberts comes to readers like roots still carrying traces of the native soil. But these beguiling voices are crafted by sophisticated artists who shape and reinvent memory, so as to convey the singular privacy and intimacy of a child's experience and render it communicable. When you read these accounts of childhood in Penmaenmawr, Abertawe, Aberystwyth and Pwllheli, you will be drawn into a miscellany of perhaps unfamiliar places and isolated experiences; yet at the same time, a reader's own childhood will be reactivated. Individual memories bubble from sources as common as they are unique. We all alike brought nothing with us when we came here: the found world of childhood saturated our senses with a totality never later experienced or endured, for consciousness closes on an intolerable plenitude as we become 'civilised', tamed, quenched or 'mature'. The anthology offers access to something of this field of primary perception, when the natural world was seen freshly, coloured with the violence of stained glass with the first and cardinal loves and needs.

Layer upon layer of memory and reflection is built up in Dewi Roberts' selection of quoted childhoods. For all, the silver clouds of glory we arrive trailing bear a shadowy lining: many children encounter too young and with thin skin the mortality of the world and its normal cruelties. Caradog Pritchard's 'The Asylum' exemplifies this shock: the youngster is handed 'all Mam's clothes' in 'such a little parcel'. R. Gerallt Jones is packed off to boarding school in a foreign place that sounds to his untutored ear like 'Shrwsbri' (I was too): 'Diawl, diawl, diawl'.

But the children of Wales are also its parents-to-be. Many of Dewi Roberts' gleanings are tender lyrics to babies and children by their mothers and fathers. Wales is rich and courageous in daring to place the heart at the centre of its aesthetic. Our babies, as John Davies writes, give us new birth, a second chance: 'With you here, Ceri, even rain's different'. Hilary Llewellyn-Williams, Frances Sackett, Gillian Clarke, Julie Rainsbury record the complexities of mothering, with searing tenderness. The death of a child is mourned in Lewis Glyn Cothi's 'Elegy for Siôn y Glyn': "The lad loved a sweet apple / and a bird and white pebbles … Oh Mary, alas that he lies dead!" For such timeless loss there is neither remedy nor explanation.

Wales, the western nation of twin tongues and many schismatic borders, speaks to readers of all nations, in many eloquent, tender voices, tempered with humour, bordered with tragedy, from the pages of this anthology.

STEVIE DAVIES

Introduction

It is hardly surprising that writers have drawn so frequently on childhood for their creative stimulus. Dylan Thomas spoke for so many when he famously wrote;

> I like very much people telling me about their childhood, but they'll have to be quick or else I'll be telling them about mine.

The joy in relating memories of the formative years to anyone who is patient enough to listen is certainly one which I share. I vividly recall bicycling expeditions in the countryside, blackberry picking in Autumn hedgerows, visits to the seaside and waiting in expectation for Santa to arrive on Christmas Eve. But to single these things out through the filter of memory is a selective process prompted by sheer nostalgia. There were, after all, some painful aspects of my experience which I prefer not to bring to mind so readily.

I make no apology for being subjective at the outset, for I suspect that this is a widespread experience.

In this anthology, the first on the subject to appear in Wales, both the celebratory and the sombre aspects of childhood and adolescence are explored through poems, fictional extracts and items from autobiographies.

The work of Welsh writers in English predominates although the reader will also find Welsh language material in translation. In addition the work of some significant English writers, including Evelyn Waugh, Bruce Chatwin and Iain Sinclair, focusing on childhood in Wales is represented.

The anthology embraces work from the seventh century to the present day. Divided into five thematic sections, the selection encompasses some diverse perspectives on childhood experience. In the seventeenth century Henry Vaughan famously reflected on his infancy

> Happy those early dayes! when I
> Shin'd in my Angell-infancy.

Dafydd Rowlands also writes in a mood of exultation:

> Come my son,
> in your father's hand
> and I will show you the beauty
> that lives in your mother's blue eyes.

Dylan's 'Fern Hill' is, of course, one of the great poems of childhood and its inclusion was mandatory, while a further major writer Kate Roberts deals with that most eagerly awaited time of the year for any child, Christmas.

In a piece of juvenilia the twelve-year-old Wilfred Owen writes home to his mother while on holiday in the Vale of Clwyd, "I am very happy but I am not wild. We are kept under great restriction..." Memoir and reportage naturally form an important part of this book. Alice Thomas Ellis recalls childhood days in Penmaenmawr, while Kyffin Williams writes of what appears to have been an idyllic upbringing on Anglesey.

All these, and many more items in my selection, may be described as celebratory, which may leave the reader wondering what represents the less exalted experiences of growing up. Schools seems to loom large.

Emyr Humphreys deals with the daunting prospect of the school examination, while Gerallt Jones writes memorably of a boy who leaves his home on the Welsh-speaking Llyn peninsular for life in an English boarding school, crossing a border both geographically and culturally.

Evelyn Waugh's account of life at Llanaber School, which he modelled on a Welsh school where he himself taught briefly, features in one of the great twentieth-century comic novels *Decline and Fall*. The actor Kenneth Griffiths reveals how he first exercised his sense of drama in the school playground

> ...in that infant's playground of the Tenby Council School,
> I organised re-enactments of the Ben Hur chariot race.

The nineteenth century has not been neglected and apart from Kilvert, Wordsworth is also represented. There are also two accounts of the harsh treatment which Welsh children received at the hands of adults at that time. The journalist and explorer H.M. Stanley describes his experiences as a juvenile inmate of the St Asaph Union Workhouse, where he had been placed by relatives:

> Much may be done with kindness as much may be done
> with benevolent justice, but undeserved cruelty is almost
> sure to ruin them.

From roughly the same period O.M. Edwards describes his early experiences of that notorious device the Welsh Not: "...my nature rebelled against the damnable way of destroying a child's character."

This introduction is all too brief a space to refer to the riches of this anthology. I invite the reader to enjoy and be challenged by my selection of childhoods, fictional and recalled.

DEWI ROBERTS

Part One

Happy those early dayes! When I
Shin'd in my Angell-infancy

BOBI JONES
The Newborn

'Your hair is thin, and your face wrinkled,
And your body withered.
Was your travelling long? Was your journey so tiring
That you were aged by your trek
From the city of God?

'Where are you going, you young old man,
The youngest old man alive?'
I'm going to burrow like a worm
In a piece of red clay soil
And cut a little hole in it for the living.

'What soil is that, you young old man,
The youngest old man alive?'
Your heart, friend. That is one hole
That I wanted, though so full of malice,
And there I can live.

'What will you do with its sourness, you young old man,
The youngest old man alive?'
Not notice it at all. Throw flowers over it
And curl up into a compact spot
Like ointment in a wound.

('Where are you going, you gentle old man?' is the beginning of a
well-known Welsh folk-song.)

HENRY VAUGHAN
The Retreate

Happy those early dayes! when I
Shin'd in my Angell-infancy.
Before I understood this place
Appointed for my second race,
Or taught my soul to fancy ought
But a white, Celestiall thought,
When yet I had not walkt above
A mile, or two, from my first love,
And looking back (at that short space,)
Could see a glimpse of his bright-face;
When on some gilded Cloud, or flowre
My gazing soul would dwell an houre,
And in those weaker glories spy
Some shadows of eternity;
Before I taught my tongue to wound
My Conscience with a sinfull sound,
Or had the black art to dispence
A sev'rall sinne to ev'ry sence,
But felt through all this fleshly dresse
Bright shootes of everlastingnesse.
       O how I long to travell back
And tread again that ancient track!
That I might once more reach that plaine,
Where first I left my glorious traine,
From whence th'Inlightned spirit sees
That shady City of Palme trees;
But (ah!) my soul with too much stay
Is drunk, and staggers in the way.
Some men a forward motion love,
But I by backward steps would move,
And when this dust falls to the urn
In that state I came return.

EDWARD HERBERT
Perfect, Eternal and Infinite

… my infancy was very sickly, my head continually purging itself very much by the ears, whereupon also it was so long before I began to speak, that many thought I should be ever dumb. The very furthest thing I remember is, that when I understood what was said by others, I did yet forbear to speak, lest I should utter something that were imperfect or impertinent. When I came to talk, one of the furthest inquiries I made was, how I came into this world? I told my nurse, keeper, and others, I found myself here indeed, but from what cause or beginning, or by what means, I could not imagine; but for this, as I was laughed at by nurse and some other women that were then present, so I was wondered at by others, who said, they never heard a child but myself ask that question; upon which, when I came to riper years, I made this observation, which afterwards a little comforted me, that as I found myself in possession of this life, without knowing any thing of the pangs and throes my mother suffered, when yet doubtless they did not less press and afflict me than her, so I hope my soul shall pass to a better life than this without being sensible of the anguish and pains my body shall feel in death. For as I believe then I shall be transmitted to a more happy estate by God's great grace, I am confident I shall no more know how I came out of this world, than how I came into it.

… certainly, since in my mother's womb this *plastica* or formatrix, which formed my eyes, ears, and other senses, did not intend them for that dark and noisome place, but, as being conscious of a better life, made them as fitting organs to apprehend and perceive those things which should occur in this world; so I believe, since my coming into this world my soul hath formed or produced certain faculties which are almost as useless for this life as the above-named senses were for the mother's womb; and these faculties are hope, faith, love, and joy, since they never rest or fix upon any transitory or perishing object in this world, as extending themselves to something further than can be here given, and indeed acquiesce only in the perfect, eternal, and infinite.

DAFYDD ROWLANDS
I Will Show You Beauty

Come, my son,
to see the reasons why you were conceived
to know why you happened.
I will show you the beauty of the breath breathed into you,
I will show you the world
that is a richness of acres between your feet.

Come, my son,
I will show you the sheep
that keep the Gwryd tidy with their kisses,
the cow and her calf in Cefn Llan,
foxgloves and bluebells
and honeysuckle on a hedgerow in Rhyd-y-fro;

I will show you how to fashion
a whistle from the twigs of the great sycamore-tree
in the incomparable woods of John Bifan,
how to look for nests on the slopes of Barli Bach,
how to swim naked in the river;

I will show you the thick undergrowth
between Ifan's farm and the grey Vicarage,
where the blackberries are legion
and the chestnuts still on the floor;

I will show you the bilberries thick
on the scattered clumps of mountain moss;

I will show you the toad
in the damp dusk,
and the old workings beneath the growing hay;

I will show you the house where Gwenallt was born.

Come, my son,
in your father's hand,
and I will show you the beauty
that lives in your mother's blue eyes.

FRANCES SACKETT
Newly-delivered mother

You will learn it very slowly –
The craft of motherhood.
No sage has taught you anything
That comes as new as this.
The baby swathed in cloth beside you,
Cocooned in light, is god-like;
Still sailing from its amniotic berth.
And by the way you lift
Your hand to touch –
But not quite touch,
And by the way
The fragile air between you
Whispers its seduction,
The world is love – all love.

SIÂN JAMES
Receiving the Adopted Child

… when the children were in bed, I received the summons I
expected to No.9 and that was much better than puzzling and
worrying and waiting for a phone call. I found Carole's state of
panicky ineptitude rather endearing, Walt's newly assumed role
of infant psychologist not.

'Piaget,' he said as I went in, raising his head and indicating
his large book. 'Now he regards learning and development as
an active process, the child taking into himself from his envi-
ronment whatever he needs and can assimilate at any particular
stage, so that the task of parent becomes one of trying to understand the process taking place in his mind and providing him
with appropriate...'

'Someone described the consciousness of the new-baby as a
great blooming confusion,' I said, trying to keep my end up.

'William James,' Walt said. ' "One big blooming confusion"; of course William James is old hat by this time. Have you ever thought how…'

Carole signalled to me behind Walt's back. 'Excuse us a minute, Walter.'

She led me upstairs and into the room which they'd been decorating and redecorating for the last two years. At present it had white walls, white broderie-anglaise curtains and lamp shades, pale grey vinyl tiles, forget-me-not blue rugs, several very large soft toys which no baby would be able to lift for at least two years, a cot swathed in white tulle, pale yellow chest and cupboard and bath and toilet basket.

She stood by the door looking stricken.

I half expected a frightful confession: the baby wasn't up to the nursery, he didn't look like they did in the adverts, she couldn't seem to take to him, but no, all she did was utter a small sound, something between a sigh and a gasp, and lead me to the cot.

And there he was, hardly raising the snow-white covers; a tiny head on the pillow, a tiny hand. 'He's beautiful,' I said. I couldn't really see him in the dimmed light but he was beautiful all right.

She touched my hand and whispered very softly, 'Timothy.'
'What?'

'Timothy. As soon as I saw him I knew he was more of a Timothy. What do you think?'

I got closer to him, so close that Carole got nervous and pulled me back.

I nodded my head vigorously and she took me out of the room.

'He's beautiful,' I told Walt.
'What's that?'
'He's beautiful.'

'Oh come, come, Tessa. You can't really pretend that a human baby, ten days old, has any pretensions to *beauty*. Come, come.'

He was as delighted as she was.

Walter was further explaining the concept of what Piaget called sensorimotor intelligence when the first wail sounded. One advantage of having a baby in hospital is that you get, in a week or ten days, fairly used to the crying, fairly inured. Carole, of course, was totally uninured. She sprang to her feet and said, 'I don't feel I can cope,' and burst into tears and Walt started to mumble, 'But all the early satisfactions are ... er ... All we have to do at the moment is to take the bottle from the bottle-warmer and ...'

'Nappy!' Carole shrieked, her hand on her heart, her voice and manner like a tragedienne crying 'serpent'.

'Look, I'll do it,' I said, 'I'm used to it.' And we all went upstairs.

HILARY LLEWELLYN-WILLIAMS
When My Baby Looks at Trees

When my baby looks at trees he sees
the wind's shape;
his face becomes still
as the branches sway and dip
for his delight, as the bright
sky dances through. He stares,
his nose twitches at leaf
and resin, sour bark, sweet earth,
the juices in the wood.
If he could climb trees
he'd be out of my arms and up
in the creaking heights
laughing among the leaves;
and his white hands move jerkily
trying to touch. What he sees
is the glow of the sap as it spreads
out and upwards, the shine
of the tree's breath.

23

His eyes widen and darken
and lighten to green;
a smile brushes his mouth
and cheek, and a look
passes light between him and the tree.
He is close in my arms, but apart.
When we turn to go
his skin smells of forests, he holds
his face to the wind.

JOHN DAVIES

For a small daughter

(i)   With you here, Ceri, even rain's different:
released at last, pushed out on its slide,
each surge down the easy sky is sent
scudding aslant fast to earth on a ride
soon levelled-out. This puddle's surface
is all unseen fish – trembling water runs
away as they dive. They leave no other trace.
Amongst the grass, look, shining buttons.

And I remember, through a splashed pane
earlier, watching swallows tighten the wire,
ready to be aimed straight through the rain
south at a new world somewhere drowsily afire.
Envious, till now I'd forgotten how best changed
perspective is: by our sharing rearranged.

(ii)   Your footsteps
wash around you;
at their edges
silence scuttles.
Day has gone out
like a tide

and here
in the dark pool
silence seems a crab.

    Invisible in shadow
    it inches in.

    But listen,
    footsteps are here
    lighting the dark,
    and new voices
    empty the pool.
    All this dry land,
    this new path!

        Look, silence is
        just a thin shy cat.

TONY CURTIS

The Infants' Christmas Concert

A moment of hush, held breath –
the fairies and robbers, the soldiers
and dancers are in position
– then the piano begins.
This sounds otherworldly,
each note a drop of water falling distantly.
Angels swallow trumpets,
a robot trips and turtles in his cardboard shell;
the ballerina crumples and cries.
They may not know why, but still
perform for us the pattern of sentiment,
superstition and love: we sigh,
smile, laugh and applaud.

'The Rich man gave them a bag of gold
and everyone cheered on the day
the church had a new bell.'
The couple are starched in best white –
as the singing swells, they marry
and claim their gold.
It is intensely sad and fleetingly
realises the ghosts of our innocence.

Flashlights – the year's frozen
for this instant.
Keep that – don't move – stay there,
stay somewhere like that forever.

It all builds to The Nativity:
Joseph, Mary and the three glittering Kings
change without age, time after time.
Only the baby Jesus doll remains,
a scarred and worn wooden face held magically
fresh each year in the laundered swaddling.
The audience – parents and children in arms,
grandparents and neighbours, point and giggle,
there's a glow and, finally, we all sing.

This has worked some sort of renewal,
some sort of ending.

TREZZA AZZOPARDI
Fran's Treasures

They all ignore Luca: she is tethered to the pram. The harness is blue and has a lamb frolicking on the front, which Luca has drenched with dribble. Two metal hooks clip on to two rusted rings at either side of the hood. She pulls at the rings, and yells, and smears her face with her sticky fist. Fran has been told to watch her; but Fran has gone Walkabout. She's got a box of England's Glory in her pocket. Inside are three pink-headed matches. She's heading for The Square.

We live at Number 2 Hodge's Row. Between Number 9 and Number 11 is an alleyway which leads on to a hopeless patch of asphalt called Loudoun Place, but which everyone calls The Square. Fran goes there a lot, sidling along the alleyway until she reaches open space. The Square is a rectangle of nothing. There used to be swings and a see-saw, but now all that's left is an iron climbing frame and a strip of battered grass. Fran explores. She likes it: better than wiping snot from Luca's nose; better than sitting on the low kerb and watching Celesta play that impossible game: better than waiting for Rose to find an excuse to hit her.

There are treasures here, stashed along the edge of The Square where scrub grass ends and gravel begins. Fran studies the ground minutely, her boots marking a careful path between the dog-shit, broken bottles, coils of rusted wire, fluttering chip-papers. The asphalt shimmers with shards of glass; green, blood-brown, clear as ice. She collects the best shapes and places them carefully in the pocket of her gymslip. Today, Fran has the matches. She strikes one and holds it to her face. A rush of phosphorous stings her nose. Crouching now, she strikes another. Fran loves this sweet, burning scent. She licks the sandpaper edge of the matchbox. A tang of spent fire.

Under her bed, Fran keeps a red oblong box. It used to have chocolates in it, and smells like Christmas when she prises off the lid. But now the plastic tray holds all her jewels from the Square: jagged slips of sapphire; worn lumps of emerald; a single marble with a twisted turquoise eye. To mark my arrival, she has begun a secret collection which she stows in a cigar box my father has given her. Not glass this time, but an assortment of cigarette stubs she picks up, when no one is looking, from the pavement outside our house. Tipped or untipped, flaky grey, or smooth menthol white. Some are crushed flat with the weight of a heel, others are perfectly round and lipstick-smeared. Fran holds each butt to her nose before she hides it away.

JULIE RAINSBURY
Daughter

She stands
flimsy in white lawn
laced and tucked
precious
as a christening gown.
Her web of hair
crazes light
across the counterpane.

Daughter –
a blood word
fills my mouth,
empties the room.

Tonight again
she came between us,
high-stepping
on wax toes,
unwound sheets
and slithered
cold into our bed.

I can't reach beyond her.
My outstretched hand
rests on a chill
of feathered breathing.
She is close
and you
are on the other side.

JAMES WILLIAMS
The Royal Beverage

My earliest recollection goes back to the hay harvest at our neighbour's farm when I was 4 years and 3 months. I cannot lay claim to the incredible memory feats of Compton Mackenzie, but I still remember this harvest time vividly, for I was allowed to carry a small jar of beer, and a cup, to the men working in the haggard and hayfields. I had served one lone worker with his drink, when curiosity made me taste the beer. I found it palatable, and so drank more, and again more, and then some, with the inevitable consequence of passing out into drunken oblivion. I was discovered fast asleep against a cock of hay – and was taken home to sleep it off. Apparently there were no ill effects, but later that summer, I was drunk again after helping Marged our neighbour, with the honey and the mead. I swallowed off and on, lots of very good honey – and drank sip after sip of the delicious mead. I knew it was the heavenliest beverage I had hitherto tasted, but my experience was about as limited as my discretion. Then suddenly I said I was going home, only two small fields away, for I was being enveloped by a billowing cloud of nausea. I was only halfway home when I began to vomit, and for a time apparently could not stop – and then I passed out. Marged who had anxiously watched my erratic homeward progress, rushed to salvage me. She was very concerned. To this day I do not like honey, and mead not at all, despite the fact that it was a royal beverage among the early Welsh.

CLIFFORD DYMENT
1 Ashwell Terrace

The house in which we lived at Caerleon was No. 1, Ashwell Terrace, one of a row of cottages that have since been condemned. My father took it because it was cheap – and because he was married, young, and a carpenter only just starting in business as a cabinetmaker. I remember that when I played on the bit of pavement outside I could look right through the cottage as though it was a telescope, through the front door seeing the back garden so close I was afraid of being stung by bees. The reason was that the cottage was only one room wide – there was one room downstairs for cooking, eating, and living in, and one room upstairs for all of us to sleep in.

There was no gas in the house: cooking was done on an open fire or in an oven at its side heated by hot embers, the embers being scraped with a steel rake from the fire to a space under the oven. For lighting we had an oil lamp which stood in the middle of a beautiful pear-wood table made by my father. That oil lamp was a beauty, too: made simply to be practical it was as graceful in profile as a piece of Samian ware. Its brass curved sides were as full of little squares and circles of reflected daylight as a polished bed-knob, and through its globe of translucent porcelain you could see shadowy images of the furniture on the other side of the room. It was my father's job to light the lamp in the evening. To me this was a ritual and a spectacle that invested him with priestly power and glory. He held a match to the wick and the wild wick snatched the flame from his hand and threw it up in the air and bounced it on the floor and hurled it up to the ceiling and flung it from wall to wall: it was a rough and playful exhibition of the eternal conflict between the forces of light and darkness. Majestically my father turned the lamp's brass wheel and the romping flame was hauled instantly back into the lamp like a tiger into its cage: the ceremony, short, brilliant, and daunting, was over. Now a cone of sunshiny radiance hung placidly from the lamp to the floor, and until it was time for me to be put to bed I scrambled about in a bell-tent made of light.

In the daytime I played in the back garden, where my father grew leaves. There were millions, billions, trillions of them. Leaves were my ceilings, walls, partitions: they pressed me down and shut me in, and when I resisted they tugged at my hair, slapped my face, pushed themselves up the legs of my short trousers, sealed my nostrils, gagged my mouth, tolled at my ears, jazzed before my eyes; and sometimes my forehead smarted and ached from the brutal rebuff of wood as a branch denied my thrusting head. All the same, I liked the leaves, and spent hours in the thousands of acres where they grew, breathing foreign green air and getting tipsy on sappy, fruity smells.

After these exotic holidays in the leaves I made my way back to everyday life by staggering across our living-room to the street. It wasn't a street really – it was more of a lane. In it there was our row of cottages, whitewashed and blue-roofed, the white walls, stained, broken, and mildewed, but seen by me now through a haze of years that gives them a dairy sweetness; and alongside them were the few flagstones of pavement, then a dirt roadway, then a hedge with a wicket gate, and then beyond the hedge, as far as I could see, nothing – though a grown-up could have looked over the hedge and viewed fields and beyond them Tyn Barlym mountain hunched low to let the clouds pass over.

I wasn't the only child in the lane. There was my younger sister Susie, and several other girls and boys busy with various occupations – chalking faces and 'Follow this line' on flags and bricks, gathering the dust of the road between their hands into little heaps shaped like children's drawings of mountains, chasing each other, pouring water from a tin teapot into tin teacups, closing eyes and counting ten, swopping licks of lollipops.

One of these children was a mystery to me. She was thin and white and ragged and hare-lipped, and she talked in grunts like an animal because she was deaf and dumb. She was always asking my mother, in her pig-speech, for something to eat. And my mother gave her something – slabs of yellow cake with mice droppings on it. I was fascinated by the monstrous child and amazed to see her eating her filthy food with such relish. It wasn't until many years afterwards that I discovered that the food my mother gave her wasn't something the mice had been on, but was caraway seed cake. Today I'm inclined to avoid cake and bread containing caraway seed.

This same girl sometimes earned a penny by taking Susie and me out in our pram. One day she stopped the pram in the middle of Caerleon Bridge and, lifting me out, held me as far over the side of the bridge as her arms could reach. At first I didn't mind – this unusual view of the world was interesting. Then, missing the support of the pram under my back, feeling all of me dangling from a point just under my armpits, I looked below. When I saw nothing but air, and deep at the bottom of the air the River Usk like a hurrying road, I was terrified. I screamed and struggled. The girl was taken by surprise and I began to slip. Instinctively she tightened her grip so that as I descended my arms hit her clutching hands with a jolt and were jerked upwards. I now screamed with pain as well as fear. Scared, the girl pulled me back and bundled me into the pram. I cried all the way home. When my mother asked for an explanation of my crying the girl, of course, couldn't give one; neither could Susie, for she was too young; and my power of speech was inadequate to describe what I had felt and seen. But whenever the deaf-and-dumb girl wanted to take me out again I protested with screeches, sobs, and rages: neighbours commiserated with my mother for having a difficult child.

SIÂN JAMES
Feeling Like Goldilocks

I remember having a beautiful china doll one Christmas and running along the tiled passage with her in my arms, although my mother had told me over and over again that I was only to play with her in the dining room where there was a carpet. Of course I fell over and her face was smashed to pieces and of course I cried and cried until I had no more breath.

After a decent interval my mother rescued the clothes – white silk dress, green knitted jacket and bonnet – and put them on an old rag doll, Kitty Fawr, who had once belonged to my sister Mair, an ugly doll with painted lips and eyes and strands of thick black wool for hair. Naturally I threw her to the other side of the room. Later, though, I was sorry I'd been cruel and picked her up and nursed her – and eventually became fond of her. Which was just as well, because I didn't get another china doll for several years.

In the winter Bob and I went to bed with a little oil lamp; she, of course, deputed to carry it up the two flights of stairs. When it was very hard weather we had a Valor stove which cast patterns like bright orange doilies on the ceiling. Sometimes Tib would sneak up and have a nap at our feet, but we could never persuade her to stay long; she was a busy cat with a hundred and one things to attend to.

I remember the summer when I was first allowed to go to meet my sister Bob from school, I think this was when I was getting on for four. One afternoon I'd set off too early and since it was very hot, I sat down to wait for her on the grass verge outside the nearer farm (there were two farmhouses fronting the lane to Llanbadarn, Brynamlwg and Cefnllan, this one was Brynamlwg) and soon I was overwhelmed by sleep. I woke up to find a little girl staring down at me. It shouldn't have been a particularly frightening experience, but somehow it was. Feeling like Goldilocks discovered by the three bears, I burst into tears and didn't stop until Bob arrived to rescue me.

JOHN TRIPP
The Children at Tenby

Below me the children
build sand castles – doomed medieval mounds
signifying power or stability.
For clear half a mile the structures
go up, small fingers shape turrets,
make arrow slits, dig out moats –
a company of hopeful engineers
with tin buckets and spades.

Bored and tired, as the sun's July lamp
burns out, they scuttle to the cliffs.
The evening collapses on the west shore.
Soon the sea will come to smash
their constructions, wash away
the frail evidence of human hands.
And tomorrow they will rush to build again,
and every summer tomorrow they will build
as they have done through the seasons at Tenby.

As they have done through all the seasons
                              at Tenby…

PHIL McKELLIGET
Baby Sitting
for Sam Maister

Circumstance had drawn us there to mind
A child whose four years spanned our separation.
Soft snores inaudible above as we

Sat chatting on the sofa, patching up
Our cloth of torn acquaintance, tentative
Our speech as mayflies over sullen water.

You had just that minute gone to fetch
Your photos from the car, when from above
There came such screams of terror, wild and dry,

A child was beating at the midnight sky!
'Tell us what's the matter Sam?', you said,
'What is it that you want?'. But, 'Go Away!'

Pitched like madness at our consolation.
Yet his eyes stayed shut and no tears came,
As if he fought for life and not with grief.

'I do believe he's still asleep', I said,
My syllables were soft against his screams.
You shared my wonder, moving in a little

closer to his cot, a spellbound witness.
We knelt outside his dreams, but knew we stalked
Within, transformed perhaps into a pack

Of baying wolves, we hounded down our prey,
Shrill cries confirming that we raged at will,
His childhood stories come alive to kill!

But suddenly it ceased. An eye appeared
And then a smudge of tear, 'It's alright Sam,
A dream', the child relaxing into sobs

That softened gently in voiceless sleep.
Downstairs our words resumed in whispered tones,
As if our speech might summon back his foes.

We both confessed to being thankful of
The other's presence there, and were aware
A trinity had formed – the child asleep

And we beneath sat listening for his breath –
It was a silence strident as the dawn,
Disturbed at last by voices at the door.

Part Two

Look at this village boy, his head is stuffed
With all the nests he knows, his pockets with flowers

DYLAN THOMAS
Fern Hill

Now as I was young and easy under the apple boughs
About the lilting house and happy as the grass was green,
  The night above the dingle starry,
   Time let me hail and climb
  Golden in the heydays of his eyes,
And honoured among wagons I was prince of the apple towns
And once below a time I lordly had the trees and leaves
   Trail with daisies and barley
  Down the rivers of the windfall light.

And as I was green and carefree, famous among the barns
About the happy yard and singing as the farm was home,
  In the sun that is young once only,
   Time let me play and be
  Golden in the mercy of his means,
And green and golden I was huntsman and herdsman, the calves
Sang to my horn, the foxes on the hills barked clear and cold,
   And the sabbath rang slowly
  In the pebbles of the holy streams.

All the sun long it was running, it was lovely, the hay
Fields high as the house, the tunes from the chimneys, it was air
  And playing, lovely and watery
   And fire green as grass.
  And nightly under the simple stars
As I rode to sleep the owls were bearing the farm away,
All the moon long I heard, blessed among stables, the night-jars
  Flying with the ricks, and the horses
   Flashing into the dark.

And then to awake, and the farm, like a wanderer white
With the dew, come back, the cock on his shoulder: it was all
  Shining, it was Adam and maiden,
   The sky gathered again

And the sun grew round that very day.
So it must have been after the birth of the simple light
In the first, spinning place, the spellbound horses walking warm
  Out of the whinnying green stable
   On to the fields of praise.

And honoured among foxes and pheasants by the gay house
Under the new made clouds and happy as the heart was long,
  In the sun born over and over,
   I ran my heedless ways,
  My wishes raced through the house high hay
And nothing I cared, at my sky blue trades, that time allows
In all his tuneful turning so few and such morning songs
  Before the children green and golden
   Follow him out of grace,

Nothing I cared, in the lamb white days, that time would take me
Up to the swallow thronged loft by the shadow of my hand,
  In the moon that is always rising,
   Nor that riding to sleep
  I should hear him fly with the high fields
And wake to the farm forever fled from the childless land.
Oh as I was young and easy in the mercy of his means,
   Time held me green and dying.

R.S. THOMAS
Farm Child

Look at this village boy, his head is stuffed
With all the nests he knows, his pockets with flowers,
Snail-shells and bits of glass, the fruit of hours
Spent in the fields by thorn and thistle tuft.
Look at his eyes, see the harebell hiding there;
Mark how the sun has freckled his smooth face
Like a finch's egg under that bush of hair

That dares the wind, and in the mixen now
Notice his poise; from such unconscious grace
Earth breeds and beckons to the stubborn plough.

KATE ROBERTS
Begw's Real Christmas

Three nights to Christmas, the very night to which Begw had been looking forward for weeks. She didn't really like Christmas, especially Christmas Eve. There wasn't much fun in looking forward to Christmas when you had to go up on a platform and recite such silly verses as

> I'm taller than my dolly
> And Daddy's taller'n me,
> But Daddy isn't growing now,
> Nor Dolly, don't you see?

Of course everybody knew that she was bigger than any doll – she hadn't one of her own – and that her father was bigger than she was. Besides, she never called her father 'daddy'. What if she forgot her lines, like last time, and got scolded by her mother? Or what if her petticoat came down, as Lisi Jane's did? She could see the audience staring at her as if they'd been terrified by a lion, only because she had forgotten her lines, and her mother's lips kept moving as they repeated the words. But it was too late, she had completely forgotten them. And just because the adjudicator had been so kind to her, she had burst into tears. Suppose it all happened again, the day after tomorrow?

Tonight everything was grand, this was her real Christmas. She was allowed to stay up after the other children had gone to bed, and Bilw was coming – Bilw who never looked cross, always laughing. Bilw who asked 'Where's Begw?' as if he'd searched the whole world to find her.

She sat by the fire, all expectations, biting her nails while her mother's back was turned to lay the table. The smell of beeswax filled the kitchen, the furniture shone brightly, and the blue and red tiles on the floor had been rubbed with a soapy cloth until they were dark. At the far end of the kitchen, the shadows spread like an eagle with wings out-stretched. Behind the shadows, photographs of grandparents, uncles and aunts, framed elegies of members of the family who had spent many Christmases in their graves. And still further back, in the dark bedroom, the younger children dreaming vaguely about Christmas and about the old man coming down the chimney with a sack on his back. They weren't afraid of the eisteddfod. They weren't old enough.

Above the table and the supper dishes hung the canary's cage, swinging to and fro and moving its fretted shadows from the sugar basin to the bread and butter plate; Dick the canary with his head on one side watching them. A blaze of fire in the grate, the red glow creeping towards the cinders piled high up the chimney. On the new mat, a white sugar sack spread the brightness of the fire still further into the room. In the peathole by the side of the oven the cat slept, curled into a ring. From the curtainpole hung two model yachts, the only toys that had survived the years, and that because they were expensive presents from wealthy relations. Outside, the wind rose and fell periodically, and its note seeped into the house like a sick man's sighing.

Old Dafydd Siôn had already arrived and was sitting in the armchair. To Begw he was just nobody, nothing more than an old greybeard, toothless, who told stories and looked at her as if she wasn't there. Sometimes he looked right through her, without smile or frown, just looking at her and poking her in the chest and growling a 'Boo!' as if he was trying to frighten her. She was well used to this. When she looked at his face, his cheekbones rising like red apples under his eyes as he ate, she wanted to laugh. But she hated to see that teardrop at the corner of his eye, like a drop of rain on the window frame.

Soon, Aunt Sara came in like a ship in full sail and stood in the middle of the kitchen floor, her face very clean and her hair drawn tight under her hat. Begw knew that she had lots of things under her shawl, and she began to unload them on the table; apples, oranges, handkerchiefs. The same things, every year. But no... something else came out, wrapped in tissue paper, a scarf for Begw. This was the first time she's had anything like this – it had always been a handkerchief – but when you wore this, everybody could see every bit of it, a white scarf with cross-stitch. She put it over her shoulders, smelt it and nuzzled into it.

That moment, the wind whistling through the door and Bilw stood in the shadow saying 'How are you tonight, and where's Begw?' She ran towards him and led him to the settle. He was so tall that when he came to the chimney beam above the open fireplace he had to bend down. He took off that cap of his with its earflaps and held his hands to the fire. Begw gazed at him. He looked so neat in the coat and waistcoat he wore on week-day evenings, with his corduroy trousers. His face so bright, his eyes shining, his teeth so fine. Pity he chews tobacco, she said to herself.

EDWARD THOMAS
The Tylwyth Teg

There was, says the story, at a small harbour belonging to Nefyn, some houses in which several families formerly lived; the houses are there still but nobody lives in them now. There was one family there to which a little girl belonged; they used to lose her for hours every day; so her mother was very angry with her for being so much away. 'I must know,' said she, 'where you go for your play.' The girl answered that it was to Pin-y-Wig, 'The Wig point,' which means a place to the west of the Nefyn headland; it was there, she said, she played with many children. 'They are very nice children, – much nicer,' said the child, 'than I am.' 'I must know whose children they are,' was the reply; and one day the mother went with her little girl to see the children. It was a distance of about a quarter of a mile to

Pin-y-Wig, and after climbing the slope and walking a little along the top they came in sight of the Pin. It is from this Pin that the people of Pen-yr-Allt got water, and it is from there they get it still. Now after coming near the Pin the little girl raised her hands with joy, at the sight of the children. 'Oh, mother,' said she, 'their father is with them to-day; he is not with them always; it is only sometimes that he is.' The mother asked the child where she saw them. 'There they are, mother, running down to the Pin, with their father sitting down.' 'I see nobody, my child,' was the reply and great fear came upon the mother; she took hold of the child's hand in terror, and it came to her mind at once that they were the *Tylwyth Teg*. Never afterwards was the little girl allowed to go to Pin-y-Wig: the mother had heard that the Tylwyth Teg exchanged people's children with their own.

KYFFIN WILLIAMS
Fairyland

Llanrhuddlad and Llanfair-yng-Nghornwy were a fairyland to a small boy, and everywhere I felt the presence of my dead forebears. *Taid* seemed to be everywhere and the faces of everyone, Church and Nonconformist alike, lit up at the mention of his name. Ten years, twenty years after his death, he was still the old Chancellor, and his memory was worshipped in the parish. Old men and old women would tell endless stories of *Taid* and *Nain*.

We used to visit farms for *crempog* teas and I used to eye the huge pot of melted butter, in which lurked the small round pancakes, with apprehension. I knew I could never eat enough to satisfy the farmer's wife, and always when I had consumed about six I could take no more. Unfortunately one's manhood was judged by one's capacity to down a vast number of *crempogau* and I always failed abysmally in the eyes of the parish.

'Well, well, you are no good,' complained one old body. 'Your father could do twelve, Master Johnny could do twenty

44

and your grandfather twenty-four.'

I was humiliated and hardly a member of the rector's family anymore.

'*Dduw*, Master John, only six? Well, well, you're hopeless.'

There would be laughter and cheerful goodbyes, but I crept away, a six-*crempog* boy.

It was a glorious place for a summer holiday. Gentle farms, and steep cliffs covered with gorse and heather; and in the spring the grassy slopes above the sea were coated with sea pinks and a pale-blue smoke of delicate scilla. Narrow lanes dived between high grass-topped banks that hid the gentle, munching Welsh blacks. The noise as they invisibly tore the sweet grass conjured up images of strange beasts. Sometimes they were elephants or buffaloes, bison or prehistoric animals.

The farm we liked best was Swtan. Everything was thatched there, the outbuildings, the pigsties and the squat little farmhouse with its mighty tower-like chimney at one end. 'Swtan' is a strange name, and long ago it used to be called 'Swittan', which reinforces the legend that Suetonius Paulinus landed there, for the 'w' is pronounced more forcibly in Welsh than it is in English.

When we stayed at Llanrhuddlad, old Hugh Jones lived there, as he had when my father was a boy. He was in his eighties when I knew him, a tall dignified figure with an iron-grey beard that emerged from beneath a black trilby hat. He farmed the few acres and fished in the bay below.

I remember one evening he took Dick and me out into the bay in his boat, and there, gazing toward the shore, he gave what amounted to a running commentary on the landing of Suetonius from his galleys. Under the spell of Hugh Jones' vivid and dramatic description I could see it all happening. Bearded, bronze-clad figures leaped from their galleys, centurions, infantrymen and finally the mighty Suetonius himself. There was a savage battle as my ancestors hurled spears and stones from the cliff-tops until, inevitably, a terrible massacre took place on the slopes of the Garn. My excitement was dampened by the feeling that Hugh Jones seemed to favour the Romans.

Swtan has long been deserted, and its ruins lie like the decomposing body of a rabbit, the thatch and rafters like a jumble of hair and bones.

Down at Porth Swtan there was sand and many-coloured cliffs, and deep rock pools with glorious starfish and sea anemones, while out at sea the grey shapes of the liners slipped by towards the Skerries, from where they would turn eastwards to Liverpool. Their great engines throbbed, and we waited for the wash to break on the sandy shore. There were days when a heavy sea-mist drenched and clung to the land, blotting out the comforting bulk of Holyhead mountain across the bay. The ships wailed and crept anxiously by while an air of mystery cloaked the land.

DYLAN THOMAS
An Ugly, Lovely Town

I was born in a large Welsh town at the beginning of the Great War – an ugly, lovely town, or so it was and is to me; crawling, sprawling by a long and splendid curving shore where truant boys and Sandfield boys and old men from nowhere, beach-combed, idled, and paddled, watched the dock-bound ships or the ships steaming away into wonder and India, magic and China, countries bright with oranges and loud with lions, threw stones into the sea for the barking outcast dogs; made castles and forts and harbours and race tracks in the sand; and on Saturday summer afternoons listened to the brass band, watched the Punch and Judy, or hung about on the fringes of the crowd to hear the fierce religious speakers who shouted at the sea, as though it were wicked and wrong to roll in and out like that, white-horsed and full of fishes.

One man, I remember, used to take off his hat and set fire to his hair every now and then, but I do not remember what it proved, if it proved anything at all, except that he was a very interesting man.

This sea town was my world; outside a strange Wales, coal-pitted, mountained, river run, full so far as I knew, of choirs and football teams and sheep and story-books, tall black hats and red flannel petticoats, moved about its business which was none of mine.

Beyond that unknown Wales with its wild names like peals of bells in the darkness, and its mountain men clothed in the skins of animals perhaps and always singing, lay England which was London and the country called the Front, from which many of our neighbours never came back. It was a country to which only young men travelled.

At the beginning the only front I knew was the little lobby before our front door. I could not understand how so many people never returned from there, but later I grew to know more, though still without understanding, and carried a wooden rifle in the park and shot down the invisible unknown enemy like a flock of wild birds. And the park itself was a world within the world of the sea town. Quite near where I lived, so near that on summer evenings I could listen in my bed to the voices of older children playing ball on the sloping paper-littered bank, the park was full of terrors and treasures. Though it was only a little park, it held within its borders of old tall trees, notched with our names and shabby from our climbing, as many secret places, caverns and forests, prairies and deserts, as a country somewhere at the end of the sea.

And though we would explore it one day, armed and desperate, from end to end, from the robbers' den to the pirates' cabin, the highwayman's inn to the cattle ranch, or the hidden room in the undergrowth, where we held beetle races, and lit wood fires and roasted potatoes and talked about Africa and the makes of motor-cars, yet still the next day it remained as unexplored as the Poles – a country just born and always changing.

There were many secret societies but you could belong only to one, and in blood or red ink, and a rusty pocket-knife, with, of course, an instrument to remove stones from horses' feet, you signed your name at the foot of a terrible document, swore death to all the other societies, crossed your heart that you would divulge no secret and that if you did, you would consent to torture by slow fire, and undertook to carry out by yourself a feat of either daring or endurance. You could take your choice: would you climb to the top of the tallest and most dangerous tree, and from there hurl stones and insults at grown-up passers-by, especially postmen, or any other men in uniform? Or would you ring every doorbell in the terrace, not forgetting the doorbell of the man with the red face who kept dogs and ran fast? Or would you swim in the reservoir, which was forbidden and had angry swans, or would you eat a whole old jam jar full of mud?

There were many more alternatives. I chose one of endurance and for half an hour, it may have been longer or shorter, held up off the ground a very heavy broken pram we had found in a bush. I thought my back would break and the half-hour felt like a day, but I preferred it to braving the red face and the dogs, or to swallowing tadpoles.

WILFRED OWEN
Juvenilia

Glan Clwyd,
Rhewl.
Aug. 7th 1905.

Dear Mother,

Thank you very much for the boots, which I received this morning. It has been so wet here that I changed my shoes and stockings 3 times on Saturday and Alec & I put our feet in hot water when we went to bed. Our feet were only just a little damp, & Mr Paton laughed & said they were all right, but Mrs Paton made us change. (Don't tell any one this!) At first, before we got to the farm the place was not what I anticipated, we had to go *through*, not along, a dirty, wet, muddy lane. But the farm is fine. I am very happy but I am not wild. We are both kept under great restriction. We got up a ladder onto a hay-stack in a Dutch Barn. In case you don't know what a D.B. is, I will draw one.

Well, we made little nests on the top but Mrs Paton heard us moving the hay & soon called us down. (Mr P. laughed). I am asked to thank Mr. Owen for the f.rod. It is useless now! We cannot fish!! No lisence!!! Is it not sad!!! Alec's Uncle broke my rod, it is mended now. He was fishing this morning when a river bailiff came up and told him something about how to fish, thinking he had a lisence! You have to pay 15 or 16 shillings for 1 to fish I think. This is a filthy letter, all blots. Thank Mary and Colin for their letters. I slept in chair bed 1st night but I do not now I sleep with Alec.

From your loving
Wilfred.

T.H. JONES

A Storm in Childhood

We had taken the long way home, a mile
Or two further than any of us had to walk,
But it meant being together longer, and home later.

The storm broke on us – broke is a cliché,
But us isn't – that storm was loosed for us, on us.
My cousin Blodwen, oldest and wisest of us,
Said in a voice we'd never heard her use before:
'The lightning kills you when it strikes the trees.'
If we were in anything besides a storm, it was trees.
On our left, the valley bottom was nothing but trees,
And on our right the trees went halfway up
The hill. We ran, between the trees and the trees,
Five children hand-in-hand, afraid of God,
Afraid of being among the lightning-fetching
Trees, soaked, soaked with rain, with sweat, with tears,

Frightened, if that's the adequate word, frightened
By the loud voice and the lambent threat,
Frightened certainly of whippings for being late,
Five children, ages six to eleven, stumbling
After a bit of running through trees from God.
Even my cousin who was eleven – I can't remember
If she was crying, too – I suppose I hope so.
But I do remember the younger ones when the stumbling
Got worse as the older terror of trees got worse
Adding their tears' irritation to the loud world of wet
And tall trees waiting to be struck by the flash, and us
With them – that running stumble, hand-in-hand – five
Children aware of our sins as we ran stumbling:
Our sins which seemed such pointless things to talk
About to mild Miss Davies on the hard Sunday benches.
The lightning struck no trees, nor any of us.
I think we all got beaten; some of us got colds.

It was the longest race I ever ran,
A race against God's voice sounding from the hills
And his blaze aimed at the trees and at us,
A race in the unfriendly rain, with only the other
Children, hand-in-hand, to comfort me to know
They too were frightened, all of us miserable sinners.

DANNIE ABSE

A Visit from Uncle Isidore

It was a winter's evening; Sidney was blowing on his hands. 'No
more school till Monday,' said Sidney. It was silly to come home
from school tea-time with the lamp-posts lit to keep away the
ghosts. It was that cold: in the middle of the road, steam rose
from a drain. We stood there, looking downwards, watching the
steam rising. 'It's the devil smoking his pipe,' I said.

Adam and Eve and Pinch me
  Went down to the river to bathe.
Adam and Eve got drownded
  Who do you think was saved?

A policeman came round the corner and we ran and we ran and we ran.

'You don't believe in Christmas, do you?' Sidney said to me.

'What's it like to be Jewish?' asked Philip.

''S'all right,' I said.

'What's the difference?' demanded Philip.

'They puts 'ats on when they pray, we takes them off,' Sidney said.

'It's more than that, their blood's different,' said Philip, 'makes their noses grow.'

'Megan's coming round our house this evening,' I interrupted, making a face. Sidney and I didn't like girls because they wore knickers and Megan was especially silly. Lots of things were silly. Girls were silly, Miss Morgan our school-mistress was silly, washing behind the ears was silly, going to bed early was silly. Now Philip was silly, because he didn't know what it was like to be Jewish. It wasn't anything really, except on Saturdays. We walked down the street wishing for snow and letting our breath fly from our mouths like ectoplasm. Soon it would be Christmas holidays, and presents and parties. The shops were crowded with voices. We pressed our noses against the window-panes, breathed, and wrote our names with our fingers on the misted glass. 'Leo loves Megan,' I wrote. It was all cotton wool in the windows, and the smell of tangerine peel, and a man with a long white beard.

'There's daft, i'n' it?' said Phillip 'Look, Father Xmas!'

'Where do flies go in the winter-time?' asked Sidney suddenly, and we all laughed sharing a secret.

When I arrived home, my brother Leo was squeezing a blackhead from his forehead; then he combed his hair.

'Megan Davies,' I shouted at him. 'Megan Davies.'

'Do your homework,' he said.

'Who loves Megan Davies?' I cried.

He hit me harder than he meant for I fell against the wall and a bruise came up like an egg on my head.

'Put some butter on it,' my brother said, 'and stop crying.'

'Bloody, bloody, bloody,' I screamed at him.

'Now then, enough of that,' he thundered. But the front door bell rang and he thought it was Megan, so I was given a penny to shut up.

It was only Uncle Isidore... I don't think I've told you about him. I'd like to tell you. Of course, he's dead now, but I remember him quite well. He's become a sort of symbol really. You know, my parents still live in Wales, but we children have grown up and left home – as much, that is, as anybody can ever leave home. Anyway, when old Dafydd Morgan comes round the house at Cardiff these days, he and my parents get to talk about the kids.

'And what about Wilfred, your eldest son?' Old Morgan asks.

'All right,' says my father, 'not just an ordinary doctor but a psychiatrist.'

'Fancy,' says Morgan, 'Wilfred not just an ordinary doctor! Now my son Ianto, 'e 'ad the gift do you know, just like his mother before she caught pneumonia, before she was... exterminated, God rest her soul.'

'And Leo, my second son,' interrupts my father.

'Ah yes, Leo, Leo, there's a boy for you,' smiled Morgan.

'A boy in a million. Very spiritual. And a credit to you; goes to chapel, I mean synagogue, regular, I understand.'

'A solicitor, Mr. Morgan, very clever!'

'Yes, very clever. Fancy, a solicitor! A very spiritual solicitor, I should think. Pays, I always think, to go to chapel – I mean synagogue. The connections do you know? Apart, of course, as a remedy for the spirit. But what about your third son, the youngest?'

'Our third son, Dafydd Morgan,' says my mother, 'is no good. Won't do any work.'

'Just like Uncle Isidore,' exclaim my father and mother, in unison, lifting up their hands hopelessly.

'Fancy,' says Morgan. 'Now my son Ianto...'

Uncle Isidore wasn't exactly an Uncle. Nobody knew his

exact relationship to the family; but my parents called him 'Uncle', and my cousins called him 'Uncle', and my uncles called him 'Uncle'. He used to visit our home regularly, once a week, to collect his half a crown and eat a bit of supper. He went around all my relations' houses to receive a silver coin and grumble. It wasn't even as if he were a religious man. He just lived that way and the rest of the time he would read at Cardiff Central Library, or return to his dingy bed-sitting-room and play his violin. Not that he was a competent musician. On the contrary, he would scrape the easy bits and whistle the difficult phrases. That was his philosophy and his life.

BARBARA HARDY
Swansea Sands

The first wild place you could go to without grown-ups, first with big children, then your peers, then on your own, was Swansea Sands. To go down the sands was to go anywhere between the old West Pier, by the docks, and Blackpill. The sands were lovely to look at, dark brown from the tide or yellow in the sun, but littered and polluted with trippers' rubbish, mud dredged up from the Channel, and sewage. The bay curved from the derelict West Pier to the three points of Mumbles Head, and the Mumbles train's twin carriages moved all day between the two points. The first boats you knew by sight were the dredgers, the tugboat and the pleasure-steamers that crossed to Ilfracombe or round the Gower coast for evening cruises. I remember going once with my mother and brother, leaning over the side, seeing a fish, and being proud of not being sick. It was calm as a millpond, my mother said, but I knew I wouldn't have been sick even if the waves had been mountainous, as they were in Mother's stories about Father's storms. I boasted of being a good sailor, savouring the phrase. Though the sea wrecked my parents' marriage, my mother would say, 'The sea's in your blood'. This was confirmed when

I recited Masefield's 'Sea-Fever', misquoting, like everyone I've ever known who has quoted from the poem, 'I must go down to the sea again', improving on the archaic and affected, 'I must down to the seas'. Having a father who was a sailor was romantic, though I wished he was a captain not a chief steward. And after a while, when I got used to missing him, I wanted to be like my friends and have a father at home. I didn't want to be different. I wished my mother was happy.

The big sewage pipes ran at intervals into the sea, emptying their contents at high water, concluding in brown but sea-smelling pools when the tide was out. We were told not to paddle in those pools, but the pipes were lovely for playing. You could run along the sand and spring up on to their high sides, to balance, jump and fool around, then jump off the end. The beach was threaded with little streams, clean and running, nameless except for Vivian Stream and the river that ran down Clyne Valley to become Blackpill. We played round the old pier, but paddled and tried to swim in the more salubrious regions near the Slip and Brynmill. Swansea Bay was really no good for bathing. At high water you could get deep enough quite quickly, and there were no dangerous gullies or pools or under-tow or currents, but the water was never clear. All kinds of bits and pieces floated round you. And at low tide you walked for miles to get even thigh-deep, plodding patiently, lifting your legs high in and out of the squish, feeling soft, nameless ooze between your toes or hurting the soles of your feet on the ripple of hard banks. Sometimes you gave up and went back, relieved if a friend suggested it first. Though we lived by the sea and played in it, we weren't taught to swim. My uncles could swim, but only Renee out of the aunts. I doubt if my grandparents ever went in except to paddle, and my mother always regretted that she'd never learnt. I used to go to the old Swansea Baths, by Victoria Park, until they were closed some time in the war because of a polio epidemic. Once, I cut my lip on the rough bottom, trying to dive at the shallow end, and that put me off for years. You didn't learn to swim at school, but with the help of a few lessons from Ron and Walter, and a rubber ring, I learnt to float, do an erratic dog-paddle, and eventually a side-stroke which I still resort to when tired or lazy.

The beach had many pleasures. There were old lumps of peat which were the remains of ancient forests. Wood became peat and peat became coal. You could pop bladder-wort and skip with long strands of some other seaweed. You could look for shells. The best ones, always rare and now gone for good, were the exquisite ancient oyster-shells worn into transparent mother-of-pearl slivers. Mother-of-pearl was on my list of beautiful words, which I added to from time to time. It was a word that meant more than pearl, a poetry half understood. And the shells were silvery, gold, copper, rainbow, in frail saucers and half-moons. We were told how real pearls were made and searched amongst the big, thick, newer oyster-shells, still pretty ancient, because it's more than a century since the rich oyster-beds flourished which gave their name to Oystermouth, the village at the west point of Swansea Bay. You found shells of mussels and cockles and whelks too, and sometimes after the weekend you could pick up ha'pennies and pennies left in the sand by the careless, happy trippers who came down from the Rhondda in charabancs.

R.S. THOMAS
Rhodri

… how did Rhodri come into my life, I wonder? After I went to the grammar school, probably. The Penrhos Feilw family were respectable and safe enough to make friends with. Rhodri was from the town, though. He didn't speak with a pure accent. He didn't get to his feet when my mother came into the room. So Rhodri was out of favour. But to me, he was like a fresh breeze from another world. He was not one of the local yobboes, yet he had no fear of them. To me the yobboes were terrifying. They used to hide behind walls and throw stones at me. They challenged me to fight and I didn't like that. If my father had taken more part in my upbringing, things would have been different. He had seen hard times in the old sailing ships, and he could look after himself. But he was at home only rarely in comparison with the time he was at sea, and so my upbringing fell largely to my mother, with results which were not to the liking of the yobboes. But Rhodri could keep up with them like a wolf with its pack. In the winter, when I was safe in the house with the curtains drawn to keep out the night, I heard sometimes an inhuman scream outside, and the sound of footsteps running past: Rhodri and his warriors on the trail! I once dared ask if I could go out to play. My mother became angry, and with righteous scorn asked: 'What, with that lot?' I never asked again after that. I was allowed to go to school with him, though, and to come home, and even to go out for a walk with him before dark. Rhodri opened a new world to me. His head was full of the fights he had seen in the cinema. It was he who taught me that the rows of foxglove were not flowers but wave after wave of Red Indians to be felled by our weapons: stones thrown – by Rhodri at least – with devastating effect. We would play ball on the way home from school. One day I kicked the ball through the window of a house. I was going to go to the door to apologise, but Rhodri grabbed my arm: 'Come along, you idiot,' he said; and off we raced. When we reached the corner, Rhodri stopped to look. 'No one to be seen,' he said, laughing victoriously. We went on, but sure enough the next day the headmaster came to the classroom and took me to his study. The cat was out of the bag, and my parents had to pay for the window. But it was Rhodri they blamed.

They did not like me being with him, though I liked nothing better than to be in his company. His conversation was full of descriptions of the beating one of his heroes gave someone in a film. Those were the days of Tom Mix and his marvellous horse, and I occasionally got permission to go and see the cowboys and Indians chasing each other across the plains. There was one cinema which continued to show silent films after the introduction of sound in the others. There was a piano there, and I can still see the pianist playing furiously by the weak light of the film, and hear the notes getting faster and faster as the Indians overtook the cart with the blonde heroine in it. I can hear, too, the deafening applause of the town lads as the hero pushed the baddy over the edge of the cliff. And then to end the film, the heroine was waiting for him under a tree smiling radiantly. I suppose it must have been Rhodri who was responsible for my noticing girls. One of his friends sometimes came with us for a walk. I would see them turning round to look after a girl who had just passed, and then start to smile stupidly and whisper to one another. 'Why didn't you say something to her?' they asked; 'She smiled at you.' It was a frightening idea to me. I was too shy to look at a girl, never mind talk to one. And yet, the little armed god was waiting for me.

There was another house my mother used to call at sometimes out in the country. It was full of children, boys and girls. One day we were there, and while my mother was talking to their mother, one of the girls took me aside and started to talk amicably about this, that and the other. Gradually I lost my shyness and began for the first time to bask in female company. I walked home with my mother as though I was in a dream. The world had been transformed. I went to sleep seeing two black eyes sparkling at me and hearing a soft silvery voice. The little god's arrow was firmly in my heart. After that there was nothing for it but to walk along the road, hoping to meet her by accident. Morning and afternoon during the holidays I could be seen on my way past her house. But I didn't succeed in meeting her. Eventually I plucked up my courage. I went through the gate to the door and knocked; trembling inside. A maid came to the door, and told me that the family were in the orchard. I went there and found the three girls with their father who had been ill. They welcomed me in a friendly and natural fashion and I sat with them under the apple-trees with the bees humming and the birds singing and the hazy, golden summer all around us. It was heavenly! I wanted never to leave. It was sufficient just to sit there listening to their sweet voices, and glancing now and then at my sweetheart. From time to time, I would also say something, just to show how daring I was. It says a lot for that kind gentleman that he asked the great lout to stay for tea! And this went on for several months while the fever continued. The shore was deserted, the fields forgotten. There was only one road worth taking. If I went to the shore at all, it was only to write her name in the sand! I do not remember how it came to an end – if it ever did, since some hold that one's first love stays with one throughout one's life. Certainly we didn't quarrel or fall out in any way. The whole thing just gradually receded from my mind, its place taken by other things.

JOHN POWELL WARD
Genes

A duet of boys.
Limbs, sticks of the species.
Chubby and spindly knees,
No nail yet on their brows.

This fair one is loved
For his forgiving.
I could not do it, have
Such pensive

Clearance in an oval face.
The opal eyes
Accept that he knows no cause
For hurts he willingly allows,

My wood-shaving, my tiny wisp of straw.
Some man years later
May rise from a chair
And tread carpet to you, lead you

Astray, his wants to answer.
Then we'll remember
The light on your puzzled hair,
My ash-leaf, our sliver of a tree.

Darker, tiny one,
What you seem to contain
Is flesh as wit, new-laid comedian.
You looked like a laughing moon

In bouncing back light
Too young to snatch it
Like a ball, to we who pat it.
For your subtler shape we must wait

Then, little egg, fat moonlight.
If such boys are our contract
In blood, one fair one dark
And both gene mystery, how do we act

Who do not even know
Whence they came, what miracle they imply?
In our eyes prayer
Is impossible; of course we try.

RONNIE KNOX MAWER

An Historical Itinerary

Outside, in the drive, Young Boot – as Father called him despite his bald head and stooping figure – had brought along an Austin Six for Father to hire; the Clyno was being overhauled at the time. Shaking his head anxiously, Mr. Boot pronounced it fit for the journey.

'Right,' Father declared, taking the wheel, 'three of you get in the back. Constance Mary can sit in the front and map-read.

Evelyn will give us the literary connotations. That boy can keep his eye on Rosemary. And let's hope he doesn't hold us up by feeling sick as usual'.

Evelyn had a copy of Tennyson's *Complete Works* on her lap. She was known to be the cleverest member of the family and something of a linguist.

'We're now retracing the paths of the Bard,' Father instructed 'he came to this part of the country to gain inspiration for the famous *Epic of King Arthur.*'

The engine spluttered into life, Father let out the clutch and we were away.

'Craig Arthur,' Father said over his shoulder, 'the seat of Arthur. Craig in the Welsh language means a seat. Am I not right Evelyn?'

'No, Father,' she ventured.

Father's neck reddened.

'Well, what on earth does it mean?'

'A rock or crag, Father.'

'Totally irrelevant anyway,' he responded, opening up the throttle with a roar. 'The whole point is that this was where Lord Tennyson came for inspiration.'

We had passed the bridge over the Dee at Llangollen and were now on the Ruthin Road.

'We are about to gain a fine view of Craig Arthur, are we not, Constance Mary?'

He glanced sternly in her direction.

'Yes, Father. If we go right to the top of the Horseshoe Pass.'

Tension mounted as we ricocheted up the incline. I tried not to look down. Father pointed a gauntleted hand to some cliffs in the distance.

'The Eglwyseg Escarpment. Right or wrong, Constance Mary?'

'Right, Father.'

The engine, like Father, was becoming overheated. Steam rose in clouds as he pulled into the side.

'And there is Craig Arthur,' he said, indicating a prominent crag. 'That was where the poet made notes for those immortal tributes to knightly chivalry.' He adjusted his wing-collar.

'Kindly read out the relevant footnote, Evelyn,' he demanded.

We held our breath as she rustled through the pages.

'Er. It says something different, Father.'

Father let out a sigh of exasperation.

'It says here Father, that many sites in Wales are wrongly named after King Arthur.' She paused.

'Yes, yes! But just carry on reading,' she was told.

In a trembling voice Evelyn did as she was told.

'To obtain the necessary inspiration for his work on King Arthur, Lord Tennyson visited the two lakes which nestle in the mountains high above Llanberis'.

There was an ominous silence.

'And precisely how far is Llanberis from here?' Father's voiced cracked out.

There was another dreadful moment as Constance Mary put on her glasses and peered short-sightedly at the appropriate map.

'Roughly fifty miles, Father. On the A5 from Shrewsbury.'

The strain was a bit too much for me. I had to fling open the back door to excuse myself. From behind a clump of heather I watched Father, blind with fury, reverse the Austin right into a flock of sheep.

'Curse the wretched creatures,' he called out. I scrambled inside again.

'They're alright, Father,' I called out reassuringly.

'I don't care tuppence whether they're alright or not. They shouldn't be allowed to roam about in the first place. I intend to complain instantly to my friend Worshipful Brother Hopkin, Secretary of the North Wales Farmers' Association.'

It was at least a relief to have Father's mind set in another direction. In any case, there was no question for Father of his tackling an expedition to Llanberis 'in an unreliable hired car,' as he put it.

NINA BAWDEN
Evacuation to Paradise

Really, it was my mother who was the country child. Married to a marine engineer and living in a small house near the London docks, she saw the suburban landscape around her as a dreary waste and pined for the Norfolk of her childhood: the heaths, the woodland, the wide skies. Her nostalgia for a Vanished Eden infected me when I was very small and by 1939, when I was thirteen and about to be evacuated from London with my school, I was entranced by the whole concept of 'living in the country' and expected Paradise.

Oddly, perhaps, I was not disappointed (I suppose I should call it my adolescence, but thirteen-year old girls were still children then) and remember perfect happiness. My mother and my brothers had left London for the Welsh border country and, although my school was evacuated to a mining town where I had to stay with foster parents in term time, my real life (in imagination when it could not be in fact) was lived with my family, in one enormous room of an old farmhouse in a beautiful valley between Montgomery and Bishop's Castle.

The life we lived there, without electricity or telephone or running water, was probably closer to my mother's childhood memories of country life than it might have been had she chosen to find safety from the Blitz in the Home Counties. We fetched our water from the pump in the yard until the well ran dry, at which point we took the trap and a milk churn to the brook. We had one hanging oil lamp and two Tilley lamps, and candles. My mother cooked (amazingly well, I realise now) on a small tin oven on an oil stove, or on the hob of the fire. The lavatory was a privy at the end of the vegetable garden, a three-seater with a large hole, a medium-size hole and a small hole. (I hated to be seen visiting there and have been constipated all my life as a result.) We had an old battery wireless to which my mother listened, but the batteries were always running down and so the news of bombing and battles came to us very ghostly and faint, as if being transmitted from another world a long way away.

I listened with my mother sometimes but the world of the farm absorbed me to the exclusion of everything else, even concern for my father who was on convoy duty in the North Sea. Collecting eggs, shutting up the chickens that roamed free all day in the orchard, helping with the harvest – these were expected pleasures. But I was a convert to country living and, like all converts, extra zealous. I begged to be given a fork and a pile of manure, to be allowed to muck out the cowsheds and the pig sties. Cleaning out the privy was the pinnacle of my achievement in this area, though I must admit that I was paid for it: the farmer, unable to credit that a 'townie' would take up his offer, had mentioned the huge sum of five pounds. But he paid me punctiliously and took me more seriously afterwards, teaching me to drive a horse and harrow, to dip sheep and, one wonderful cold winter's night, got me out of bed to hold the lamp at a difficult birth. His arm was buried up to his shoulder inside the cow; he sweated and grunted as she threw him from side to side. He pulled until the tiny front hooves appeared, held firm in his hand, and the calf was born with a slippery rush of mucus and blood. I said, when it had risen to its tottery feet, 'This is the best moment of my whole life.' And instead of laughing, as I feared he would, my farmer friend said, 'I never get tired of it; it always gets me in the throat.'

EILUNED LEWIS

In the Granary

There was, she considered, the apple-room, a pleasant, sweet-smelling place where the sun filtered through on to rows of green and rosy apples, reached by a flight of stone steps, slippery with moss. Chased up those steps once by David, Lucy had taken a flying leap from the top, jumping into a heap of dead leaves and broken wine-bottles beneath. She had been badly cut, and hide and seek was forbidden for a whole week afterwards. No, not the apple-room to-day, she decided.

By this time she had reached the stable-yard; in the distance behind her she heard Delia's shrill cry of 'Coming!', and at that she slipped into the coach-house and up the stairs into the loft.

Now, the children's father had issued orders that no one was to climb those stairs because the roof above the coach-house was unsafe, so that a disobedient child might at any moment be precipitated with a cascade of outworn lath and plaster on to the brougham or dog-cart below, or even on to grandmother's phaeton, shrouded in dust-sheets, its upturned shafts mutely imploring. Here then was a place which not even the wise Delia or crafty Olwen would think of searching. Holding her breath, Lucy stepped lightly across the forbidden territory, an over-turned garden-seat and a disused pair of oars looming in the half-light, pushed open the door beyond and stepped into the granary: only when she had closed and bolted the heavy oak door behind her did she breathe freely.

The granary reminded her of church: there was the same raftered roof and a window cut into small, heavily-leaded panes, high up in the wall. By standing tiptoe on a corn-bin she could see through it, and there far below were the corner of the paddock and the place where the mown grass was tipped in a green pile, and the white door into the kitchen garden: yet seen from here all these things were bright, shining, unfamiliar, like the world when you stooped down and looked at it backwards between your legs; or like a day when Louisa was not in one of her scolding moods.

That day had begun badly, but as soon as the Rectory children came to tea everything was all right, and there was Louisa in her starchy, clean apron and cap, sitting behind the blue teapot and talking as though her mouth were suddenly full of plums. 'Now Master David, will you have some Jam-sandwich?' Pass the bread and butter to Miss Olwen, Lucy.' 'Have you seen our new kittens, Miss Lena? They're such pretty little things.'

How round and still the world seemed then! The blue rim on the nursery tea-service was a circle that enclosed it, and safe inside were the dim room shadowed with leaves, the white cloth, the sound of wood-pigeons in the garden, the pattern in the branches of the trees which Lucy could see from her place at table, and Louisa and she on good terms with each other.

Louisa was really very kind at times, Lucy thought, settling herself comfortably on the corn-bin. For instance, she had not laughed at all when she discovered that Lucy was always expecting God to call her, as He had called the Infant Samuel. For a long time, after hearing that story, Lucy went about listening, and when, as sometimes happened, she fancied she heard a voice she would stand still and with closed eyes and clasped hands repeat the words: 'Speak, Lord; for Thy servant heareth.' Sometimes the voice turned out to be her mother calling to Beedles; on one occasion it was Louisa herself: 'Didn't you hear me?' she asked angrily when Lucy, realising that the call was not, after all, from Heaven, had come reluctantly in from the garden. 'Why didn't you come at once?' Something prompted Lucy to tell. (Oh, how awful if David and Delia were to find out! How they would laugh at her!) Yet, because there had been so many disappointments, because she despaired of God's ever really wanting her, she had blurted out the truth to Louisa, and Louisa had suddenly enfolded her in her arms.

'Nemo-dear! You get some old-fashioned notions, to be sure!'

After that she had given up listening for God's voice, but now in the remote and silent granary, with the sound of voices calling in the distance, she fell to thinking of Him once more and decided that this would be a very good place in which to play at Church. Delia would be the congregation, a part she acted with great spirit, kneeling with fervently bent head or leaning forward from the waist, according to the character she represented. Maurice would be the organist, pulling out the stops of an invisible harmonium, and Lucy would preach the sermon and compose the hymns – both words and music. She began to invent one now, and was rather pleased with the result:

> Think, think, think,
> Of all the wrong you've done,
> Think, think, think,
> Of all the wrong you've done,
> Think, think, think...

When she grew up, she decided, she would write hymns which people would print with her name at the end, and after it the date on which she was born, as they did in Louisa's chapel hymn-book. At first this would be followed with a dash and a blank, but after she was dead there would be the date on which she died, and when Louisa herself sang the hymns in her strong, trilling voice she would remember Lucy and perhaps the tears would come into her eyes at the thought of all the times she had scolded her. That, Lucy reflected, would be very satisfactory.

GLYN JONES
On the Summit

We had sweated as we had climbed, hungry and burdened, and with hammering pulses, the steep and windy gradients near the mountain's summit; we were petulant and blown. But once on the long crest we dropped our burdens and performed in the high wind a shouting and boisterous tripudiation in honour of our achievement: we crowed like dawn-cocks: we wallowed like tingling dolphins in the showers of wind: we bit like exultant pit-ponies put out to grass: we covered the mountain's sunlit back with the patterns of our exultation and delirium, with the bedlam choreography of our dizzy eleutheromania. And then, when at last we sat down, we were silent and a little awed. There was no living soul within miles of us. There was no dwelling to be seen anywhere in the glass-like clarity of the air, not Ystrad our village nor Pencwm the town at the valley's end. Once, so Benja said, a lost boy had starved to death on these mountains. When they found his body he had eaten his hands to the bone. We all laughed again and having lit a grass cooking-fire the three of us sat laughing beside it.

To me the mountain was painter's country. Over our heads, as we cooked, large masses of lathery clouds were blown through the blue like frondent soap, silvered and convolved,

sloshing vast bucketfuls of brilliant light over our whole mountain. The majestic swimming ridge on the far side of the wide
valley rose convulsively into the sunshine; as I watched I saw it
constantly sloughing the teeming cloud-shadows off its head
and shoulders. And there, between the driven foliage of swift
shade, was the stone-quarry's amphitheatre, taken out of the hill
as it were at one bite. Benja, singing his quatrains, leaned back
against the ruined dry-built wall. He was wearing his shrunken
white-boiled holiday suit, a pair of buttoned boots, and a motor-
bike helmet. As he waited for our food to boil in the billy-can he
sang of the strange behaviour and misfortunes of eccentric local
females. He sang of his sister Mary who was working in the
dairy: and his sister Elin who was courting in Llwyn-celyn: and
his sister Liza and his mother couldn't rise her...

> For I had a sister Anna
> She could play the grand pi-anner;
> She could also play the fiddle
> Up the side and down the middle,
>   Wass you effer see,
>   Wass you effer see,
>   Wass you effer see,
> Such a funny thing before?

'On a fine day,' he said, when our counter-songs had
brought to an end his interminable stanzaic cycle, 'on a fine day
you can see all the county of Glamorgan from by here, aye.'

'And all Monmouthshire,' I said. 'You can see the fairies
dancing on Twyn Barlwm.'

'And all Carmarthenshire,' said Evan. 'You can smell the
laver-bread in Carmarthen market.'

Benja looked with dislike from one of us to the other, uncertain whom to start horsing first. But we went on and baffled
him by our fluent collaboration; we named in progressive
inconsequence Cardiganshire, where all the girls have big
noses; and Pembrokeshire, where the bugs ate the sailor; and
Breconshire where King Brychan Brycheiniog put the shovel
down. To secure the postponement of our penal thumps and
fierce retroflexions of the arm we then bestowed nonsensical

attributes upon all the other Welsh counties we could remember and the English boroughs and the transatlantic colonies where our countrymen still utter the tricky mutation of our native speech – London, Liverpool, Vermont, Scranton, Pa., and the Chubut Valley of Argentinian Patagonia.

Benja waited and our stratagem was successful. 'Don't talk so damn daft, will you?' was all he said. 'Don't talk so damn daft.'

Then he dropped his eyes, which had flickered with uncertain hostility between Evan and me, and became silent and absorbed. For the moment he appeared to be confronted with the futility of all his aspirations and enterprises. He watched in silence our dinner bubbling above the grass-and-twig fire, staring at the flames which stamped upon it or blared sideways in the breeze.

We had forgotten to bring water and we were boiling our potatoes in lemonade. Far down there under the calm curtains of the birches we had come across a limpid little stream, but Benja forbade us to take water from it. He interrupted his narrative to stop us, a tale of what he did with a live bullet he had found.

'Gudge, don't drink that,' he said, as we stood beside the stream. 'An old hag spits and bathes her bad leg in it every morning. She's got green teeth and' – here he bent down and struck the mid point of his shinbone – 'her foot is purple up till here. Come on,' he urged us, spitting into the current himself. 'There's drinking water further up.'

'What happened to the bullet after?' asked Evan.

'When my old man was out in chapel,' Benja went on, 'I fastened it in a hole in the stitching-machine and then I gave the what-you-call at the back a whang with the rasp and hammer. You ought to have heard the bang, aye, it sounded like a frigging thunderbolt, aye.'

'Did it do any harm?' asked Evan.

'No, no harm,' said Benja. 'Only it went through two doors and out through the parlour window. But my old man hasn't noticed the holes yet.'

I always wondered about Benja, he was so wayward, so boastful, rebellious, untruthful. I remembered his flow of obscenities after a calamitous examination, when he cursed the entire Welsh begetters of the infixed or post-vocalic pronouns. I remembered his zeal in collecting synonyms for the word 'brothel.' I remembered him, at a hint of salaciousness, hounding smut through the collected works of Chaucer. I remembered his endless lies to me, to Evan, to the masters, to his parents. And yet I always wanted his company. Evan and I never enjoyed ourselves so much as when Benja was with us.

FRANCIS KILVERT
Ten Miles for a Kiss

By Tyn-y-cwm Meadows to Newchurch village and in turning in at the old Vicarage garden door I heard the hum of the little school. The door under the latticed porch was open and as I went in a pretty dark girl was coming out of an inner door, but seeing me she retreated hastily and I heard an excited buzzing of voices within the schoolroom and eager whispers among the children: 'Here's Mr Kilvert – it's Mr Kilvert.' Not finding the good parson in his study I went into the schoolroom and fluttered the dove cot not a little. The curate and his eldest daughter were away and pretty Emmeline in a russet brown stuff dress and her long fair curls was keeping school bravely, with an austere look in her severe beautiful face, and hearing little Polly Greenway read. Janet and Matilda dressed just alike in black silk skirts, scarlet bodices and white pinafores, and with blue ribbons in their glossy bonny dark brown curls, were sitting on a form at a long desk with the other children working at sums. Janet was doing simple division and said she had done five sums, whereupon I kissed her and she was nothing loth. Moreover I offered to give her a kiss for every sum, at which she laughed. As I stood by the window making notes of things in general in my pocket book Janet kept on interrupting her work to glance round at me shyly but saucily with her mischievous beautiful grey eyes. Shall I confess that I travelled ten miles today over the hills for a kiss, to kiss that child's sweet face. Ten miles for a kiss.

LESLIE NORRIS
Water

On hot summer mornings my aunt set glasses
On a low wall outside the farmhouse,
With some jugs of cold water.
I would sit in the dark hall, or
      Behind the dairy window,
Waiting for children to come from the town.

They came in small groups, serious, steady,
And I could see them, black in the heat,
Long before they turned in at our gate
To march up the soft, dirt road.
      They would stand by the wall,
Drinking water with an engrossed thirst. The dog

Did not bother them, knowing them responsible
Travellers. They held in quiet hands their bags
Of jam sandwiches, and bottles of yellow fizz.
Sometimes they waved a gratitude to the house,
      But they never looked at us.
Their eyes were full of the mountain, lifting

Their measuring faces above our long hedge.
When they had gone I would climb the wall,
Looking for them among the thin sheep runs.
Their heads were a resolute darkness among ferns,
      They climbed with unsteady certainty.
I wondered what it was they knew the mountain had.

They would pass the last house, Lambert's, where
A violent gander, too old by many a Christmas,
Blared evil warning from his bitten moor,
Then it was open world, too high and clear
      For clouds even, where over heather
The free hare cleanly ran, and the summer sheep.

I knew this; and I knew all summer long
Those visionary gangs passed through our lanes,
Coming down at evening, their arms full
Of cowslips, moon daisies, whinberries, nuts,
　　　　All fruits of the sliding seasons,
And the enormous experience of the mountain

That I who loved it did not understand.
In the summer, dust filled our winter ruts
With a level softness, and children walked
At evening through golden curtains scuffed
　　　　From the road by their trailing feet.
They would drink tiredly at our wall, talking

Softly, leaning, their sleepy faces warm for home.
We would see them murmur slowly through our stiff
Gate, their shy heads gilded by the last sun.
One by one we would gather up the used jugs,
　　　　The glasses. We would pour away
A little water. It would lie on the thick dust, gleaming.

SIÂN JAMES
The Church near the Waterfall

Mrs Woodison lived in a little grey village surrounded by grey
hills where it rained every day; it was a beauty spot. The name
of the village was 'The Church near the Waterfall', but none of
them could pronounce it. She told them that the church had a
famous stained glass window and that they could go to see it if
the rain stopped, and Stephen said 'How delightful,' and they
all spluttered again. But when *Saturday Morning Roundabout*
was over, they put their anoraks on deciding to go and find the
waterfall to throw stones at it. Thomas had important letters to
write, but he promised faithfully to take them to the funfair the
next day.

First they walked down the road to the shop which had two small windows full of packets of soap powder and bought four liquorice sticks each, which was the only thing they could get with the money Mrs Woodison had given them for crisps. Then they took the path to the church, chewing contentedly and leering at one another as their teeth became more and more discoloured. 'Look at my black spit,' Joss said, gobbing at the path.

They came to a brook and Stephen said it would be bound to lead to the waterfall if they walked back against the current, but though they walked miles and miles through soaking wet grass, they didn't come to it. They came to some cows, though, who stared at them, lifted their heads and said, 'Mmm,' but kept their distance. Stephen told them not to look back at them over their shoulders because it would make them angry, but Joss and Harry couldn't help it; they liked the way they said 'Mmm' instead of 'Moo.' They both agreed that cows were much more intelligent than sheep.

A tall, thin, grey-haired woman came down the hill towards them. She stopped dead in front of them so that they had to stop too. 'Where are you going, then?' she asked them, her thin, mild voice full of surprise.

Stephen said they were going to the waterfall.

'English visitors,' she said. 'Where are you staying? At Nant Eos?' She didn't wait for an answer. 'Anyway, you're going the wrong way for the waterfall. This track only leads to Cefn Eithin, and there's no one there but me, and I'm out. But come, I'll show you the way. Now, can one of you carry this parcel for me, I wonder? Only it's very heavy. It's a old mirror with a gold frame that I'm hoping to sell in Denbigh this afternoon. Don't drop it, will you, or it'll be seven years' bad luck. Isn't this rain terrible?'

Stephen took the mirror, but however he tried to carry it, it banged against his knees as he walked.

'You'll never do it that way, *bach*.' She looked back at Martin. 'But if your friend takes one end, you'll be able to carry it between you. See if you can manage the old thing as far as the stile and then I'll take it again. Oh, that's better. Oh, you are good, careful boys. Where are you from, then? You should go to

Rhyl if the rain clears up this afternoon. I used to relish a trip to Rhyl when I was a girl. Haven't been for years now, of course. I'm too old for funfairs, but I used to love them. To tell you the truth I used to be a bit of a devil on the Big Wheel. There's nothing much to the waterfall, mind, only a lot of water from the mountain falling over some old stones. The tourists seem to like it, of course, they come in droves with their shorts and their fat thighs. It's reckoned to be one of the sights around here. But you get your mammy and daddy to take you to Rhyl as soon as the rain stops.'

They walked slowly and carefully as far as the stile. 'Oh, dear God,' she said then, coming to a sudden halt, as though receiving a personal revelation from On High. 'You're Mrs Woodison's little grandsons, aren't you?' She flung her arms round Joss and Harry, giving them a long, painful hug. 'And here's me bothering you about my old mirror and you with your poor mother gone. Give it here, do.'

She took the mirror from Stephen and Martin, propped it against her hip and tried to hug them, too, but they stepped smartly out of her way, so that she hugged Joss and Harry again for an even longer time.

'Now I go to the village this way, and you go that way to the church, and when you get there, just walk straight on and you'll hear the waterfall. And perhaps you'll stop to see the rose window in the church as well. Some people say it's the most beautiful window in Wales, it's very old anyhow. Well, I'll say goodbye. And, believe me, I'm more sorry than I can say.'

'Silly old cow,' Stephen said, his voice sounding as though he was full of cold.

'She had very stiff bones,' Joss said. 'My nose was bent against her chest.'

'I wish we were at home,' Harry said.

They all wished that, as they walked along the slightly wider path leading to the church, kicking at stones as they went. The waterfall failed to impress. They stood as close to the spray as they dared, but it was only like more rain and they were soaked already, their trainers gurgling like hot-water bottles as they walked. Martin said Niagara was the biggest waterfall in the world and Stephen said the Victoria Falls, but even that sharp disagreement didn't seem worth having a fight about. And however violently they hurled stones into the waterfall, they were simply swallowed up, making no impression at all.

They walked back towards the church, sodden and dispirited, but instead of keeping to the path at the front, they climbed up the grassy bank behind it. The rain stopped and a watery sun appeared between the dingy white clouds.

'I used to be a devil in the funfair,' Martin said, imitating the woman's nasal accent. They all laughed, delighted to have something to laugh about.

'I used to be a devil on the Big Wheel,' Stephen said. 'You get your mammy and daddy to take you to the funfair this afternoon.'

'Look at that bloody church,' Martin said after a few seconds' silence. 'Look at that bloody famous window. It doesn't look very bloody much from up here, does it? All dark and bloody dismal. Let's throw some bloody stones at it.'

Stephen should have stopped them, he knew that, but they were a long way away and he didn't really think any of them would manage to hit the window, though it was, it had to be admitted quite definitely a large one. 'Six goes each,' he said, and they scrambled back to the path to pick up stones. 'Small ones,' he added firmly, still struggling to be the responsible eldest brother.

Neither Joss nor Harry managed to hit the back of the church, let alone the window. Two of Martin's stones hit it, but bounced off. Stephen aimed five stones without success so, unwilling to be outdone by Martin, he put considerable force and effort behind his last throw, and the stone, marginally bigger than the others, went right through one of the small grey panes at the very top of the window. The sharp burst of pleasure he felt at his success was immediately followed by a sickening numbness as he saw the small round hole in the window.

'What a dumb thing to do,' he said.

'And that man saw us climbing up here,' Martin added.

'Let's go back to Granny's,' Harry said.
They walked slowly back to the village.

LESLIE NORRIS
Camping

Most weekends when the weather was good enough I used to go cycling in the mountains, usually the Brecon Beacons or the Black Mountains near the Herefordshire border. At that time, when I was about fifteen, I used to belong to the Youth Hostel Association, and so did Del Wellington and Charlie Bond, my friends. We used to pay a membership fee of five shillings a year and in return we got an enamel badge and a card to show we belonged to the Association; we were also sent a map which showed the location of all the Youth Hostels, most of them remote farmhouses, where we could stay for a night or two. Occasionally during the winter we'd plan, with the help of such a map, an immense journey through the dales of Yorkshire, unimaginably distant and foreign, knowing we'd never get there.

We knew all the hostels within possible cycling distance of our homes, although we rarely used them. Del's father had given us a heavy tent, already old, and we preferred to lug this about with us. We must have looked very odd on our three decrepit cycles – mine was rescued from the scrapyard and restored with loving care and some curious home-made fittings – all our strange equipment tied about us. Del always carried the tent on his bike, its bulk of canvas folded in an awkward sausage and slung beneath his cross-bar. It was so big that he had to ride bowlegged.

We had great times. Once we camped on a high moor in mid-Wales and I awoke in the middle of the night. I poked my head out of the tent into a moonlight whiter than frost, and all around us, still as wool, the sheep stood, hundreds of them, staring at the tent. I got back into my blankets and went to sleep and when the morning came there were no sheep to be seen anywhere. I didn't say a word about them to Del and Charlie.

I remember, too, camping near the foot of a waterfall. We hadn't meant to stay overnight, but we'd been attracted by the voice of the water, had pushed our bikes over a wet meadow towards the stream, and followed it up about four hundred yards until we reached the waterfall. It wasn't very high, perhaps sixty feet, but it was perfect. The white fall, never more than a foot wide, bent slowly over a ledge of rock and dropped without check into the pool beneath. We bathed in this pool. It was deep, cold enough to make us gasp, and the cleanest water I have ever used. It made our skins unrecognisable to us, as if a slippery layer of something had been stripped off us for the first time in our lives.

It took us quite a while to drag our gear up to the pool, and it wasn't easy to pitch our tent there, but we did it at last and went to sleep listening to the water's muted thunder. In the morning the green sun filtered down to us through the over-hanging branches of the trees over head, and through the nodding ferns on the wet rocks. I could have stayed there forever.

That year we got away as often as we could. Perhaps it was a natural restlessness, the wish to see over the next hill, and the next; perhaps we realised that time was already beginning to run out for us, that there were responsibilities we would have to recognise, as well as the attractions of more sophisticated and less perfect pleasures. Whatever it was, hardly a week went by without us moving north into the deep mountains, slowly through the little villages climbing the one road out, merrily over the bare uplands guarded by buzzards. After a while we ventured farther afield; leaving our tent behind and using the Youth Hostels.

Towards the end of July the weather turned unseasonably bad. There was heavy rain, and a brutal wind sprang up in the evenings. The last Friday was depressing and we decided at school that we could go nowhere that weekend. I got home about five and began to read, eating some food aimlessly and without savour. The doorbell rang and my mother answered it. After a little while Charlie Bond came in. He had his cycle cape over his shoulders. It was black, with a hood.

'What do you think?' said Charlie.

I looked out of the window. The rain had stopped and a faint, watery sun showed tentatively behind the clouds.

'I don't know,' I said.

'It'll be good,' said Charlie. 'The wind's dropped and it's cool enough for a fast ride. Del's coming.'

'Mrs Wellington is never going to let Del go out in this weather!' said my mother. 'There must be something wrong with her! Well, you're not going, my boy, so don't ask it.'

The way she spoke I knew it was all right, so I grinned at her and got ready. I pushed my bike outside – Charlie's was leaning against the kerb.

'Where's Del?' I said.

'I haven't been over yet,' said Charlie. 'I only said he was coming so that it would be easier to persuade your mother.'

Together we called for Del and I suppose we were on our way before six o'clock. Everything went right for us. Before we were out of town the sun was shining and the evening had miraculously cleared.

GLYN JONES
The Long Grass

In a very lonely and secret part of the woods we knew a sort of grassy platform, a flat square of turf sticking out level from the slope of the mountain, not far from the rocky cart-track that led up from the farm; past the powder-house and over into the next valley. There we had our camp, the paths up to it through the bracken blocked with mounds of dead thorn bushes. The trees were thick as a jungle around us there, and the grass was very tall; it was hard to find it because of this, and because of the deep bracken surrounding it. Although the square platform itself was covered with very close turf we always called our camp the long grass. We had built a cave on one side of the platform out of old pit tramlines; we had upended a ring of them into a sort of wigwam shape, and covered them outside with thick branches, so that we had a hut big enough to hold the four of us if it happened to come to rain. And it was handy to keep our stuff in an old bucket and a frying-pan and that, and matches and cigarettes, and Jeffy's clay pipe and tobacco.

Once on a Saturday afternoon when we got there we found half a dozen dirty kids from the British school with snobby noses and donkey-cropped heads messing about on our turf, they were out for the day and they had their fishing-nets and their homemade cricket bats and their lunch in newspaper with them. They were pulling branches out of the huge heap of kindling we always collected to keep our fire going, and they had turned the flat stones we used to sit on upside-down, showing the white grass underneath, and the worms writhing, and the wood-lice trotting about. One of them was even swaying up and down in the branches of the sloping tree Jeffy used to walk up to drink his soup in, and that made him mad. He rounded the kids up and told them this camp was private property, but now, because they had found out our secret hiding-place, they all had to join our gang. And to join they must bend over and have three whacks across their ragged arses with their own cricket bat. The kids were too frightened to refuse and Jeffy got them into line, the four of them, touching their toes. He brought the bat slowly up to the first kid's trousers and then drew it back again, getting his eye in for the clout, he did this three times, counting out loud – one – two – meaning to give the kid a real stinger when it came up to three. But he never got there. The next thing we saw was Jeffy staggering back and the bat flying out of his hand. The big fat sister of one of the kids, a girl about thirteen, had rushed mad out of the woods with her bubs jumping about in her blouse and given him a hefty welt on the side of the head that nearly put him down on the grass.

'What do you think you're doing, you big bully?' she shouted at him, red in the face and cock-eyed with temper.

Jeffy was too startled for once to say anything. She picked up the bat and came on at him with it over her head, but when she saw all the little kids scampering away into the trees in different directions, she stopped.

'Wait for me,' she shouted out after them. 'Moncrieff and Sylvester, wait a minute or you'll get lost.'

But they wouldn't stop running, they went on shouting back, 'Four-eyes', and, 'Ginger, you're barmy' at Tom and me, and she had nothing to do but run off into the woods after them.

Charley rolled on the grass helpless, and so did I, and even Tom Stiff had his mouth open wide laughing although he wasn't making a sound.

'Moncrieff and Sylvester,' I shouted to Charley, although I could hardly get the words out, and we said to each other, when we could manage it for laughing, the other kids' names that used to make us helpless – Vince and Jabez in form one, and Punter Thomas and Archie Sproule whose middle name we found out was Keepence, and the big fat Shadbolt twins with pimples and glasses next door to Charley in Grosvenor Gardens, Martha Serena and Aggie Superba. But Jeffy wouldn't laugh, he had pouted, he went off by himself sulking into the bracken because the fat girl had simpled him in front of us all.

MIKE JENKINS

The Woods

Hacked through trees
the paths raced bare
of grass and weed,
were there before we came.
Each moment became the next one
except from the clearing,
where a ledge of earth
was look-out on a farm:

its high-wire fences protecting
an orderly world outside
our gorse-roofed dwellings.
Our talk of electric charges

burning you to ash
if you dared... dash, jump,
swing... the bramble scabs
and mud-patches on knees

would seep in, to make
a map of these woods
whose names were Burma, Apache-land,
whose buzzards spied for 'Nazzis'.

Every day we died many times.
Nettle-stings more painful
than falling down and counting out:
dock leaf emblem of our tribe.

DYLAN THOMAS

Dan, Sidney, George and I

...there was a lane to the first beach. It was high tide, and we heard the sea dashing. Four boys on a roof – one tall, dark, regular-featured, precise of speech, in a good suit, a boy of the world; one squat, ungainly, red-haired, his red wrists fighting out of short, frayed sleeves; one heavily spectacled, small-paunched, with indoor shoulders and feet in always unlaced boots wanting to go different ways; one small, thin, indecisively active, quick to get dirty, curly – saw their field in front of them, a fortnight's new home that had thick, pricking hedges for walls, the sea for a front garden, a green gutter for a lavatory, and a wind-struck tree in the very middle.

I helped Dan unload the lorry while Sidney tipped the driver and George struggled with the farm-yard gate and looked at the ducks inside. The lorry drove away.

'Let's build our tents by the tree in the middle,' said George.

'Pitch!' Sidney said, unlatching the gate for him.

We pitched our tents in a corner, out of the wind.

'One of us must light the primus,' Sidney said, and, after George had burned his hand, we sat in a circle outside the sleeping-tent talking about motor-cars, content to be in the country, lazily easy in each other's company, thinking to ourselves as we talked, knowing always that the sea dashed on the rocks not far below us and rolled out into the world, and that tomorrow we would bathe and throw a ball on the sands and stone a bottle on a rock and perhaps meet three girls. The oldest would be for Sidney, the plainest for Dan, and the youngest for me. George broke his spectacles when he spoke to girls; he had to walk off, blind as a bat, and the next morning he would say: 'I'm sorry I had to leave you, but I remembered a message.'

It was past five o'clock. My father and mother would have finished tea; the plates with famous castles on them were cleared from the table; father with a newspaper, mother with socks, were far away in the blue haze to the left, up a hill, in a villa, hearing from the park the faint cries of children drift over the public tennis court, and wondering where I was and what I was doing. I was alone with my friends in a field, with a blade of grass in my mouth saying, 'Dempsey would hit him cold,' and thinking of the great whale that George's father never saw thrashing on the top of the sea, or plunging underneath, like a mountain.

'Bet you I can beat you to the end of the field.'

Dan and I raced among the cowpads, George thumping at our heels.

'Let's go down to the beach.'

Sidney led the way, running straight as a soldier in his khaki shorts, over a stile, down fields to another, into a wooded valley, up through heather on to a clearing near the edge of the cliff, where two broad boys were wrestling outside a tent. I saw one bite the other in the leg, they both struck expertly and savagely at the face, one struggled clear, and, with a leap, the other had him face to the ground. They were Brazell and Skully.

'Hallo, Brazell and Skully!' said Dan.

Skully had Brazell's arm in a policeman's grip; he gave it two quick twists and stood up, smiling.

'Hallo, boys! Hallo, Little Cough! How's your father?'

'He's very well, thank you.'

Brazell, on the grass, felt for broken bones. 'Hallo, boys! How are your fathers?'

They were the worst and biggest boys in school. Every day for a term they caught me before class began and wedged me in the waste-paper basket and then put the basket on the master's desk.

Sometimes I could get out and sometimes not. Brazell was lean, Skully was fat.

'We're camping in Button's field,' said Sidney.

'We're taking a rest cure here,' said Brazell. 'And how is Little Cough these days? Father given him a pill?'

We wanted to run down to the beach, Dan and Sidney and George and I, to be alone together, to walk and shout by the sea in the country, throw stones at the waves, remember adventures and make more to remember.

LORNA SAGE

Grandparents

… They both felt so cheated by life, they had their histories of grievance so well worked out, that they were *owed* service, handouts, anything that was going. My mother and her brother they'd used as hostages in their wars and otherwise neglected, being too absorbed in each other, in their way, to spare much feeling. With me it was different: since they no longer really fought they had time on their hands and I got the best of them. Did they love me? The question is beside the point, somehow. Certainly they each spoiled me, mainly by giving me the false impression that I was entitled to attention nearly all the time. They played. *They* were like children, if you consider that one of the things about being a child is that you are a parasite of sorts and have to brazen it out self-righteously. I want. They were good at wanting and I shared much more common ground with them than with my mother when I was three or four years old. Also, they measured up to the magical monsters in the story books. Grandma's idea of expressing affection to small children was to smack her lips and say, 'You're so sweet, I'm going to, eat you all up!' It was not difficult to believe her, either, given her passion for sugar. Or at least I believed her enough to experience a pleasant thrill of fear. She liked to pinch, too, and she sometimes spat with hatred when she ran out of words.

Domestic life in the vicarage had a Gothic flavour at odds with the house, which was a modest eighteenth-century building of mellowed brick, with low ceilings, and attics and back stairs for help we didn't have. At the front it looked on to a small square traversed only by visitors and churchgoers. The barred kitchen window faced this way, but in no friendly fashion, and the parlour on the other side of the front door was empty and unused, so that the house was turned in on itself, against its nature. A knock at the door produced a flurry of hiding-and-tidying (my grandmother must be given time to retreat, if she was up, and I'd have my face scrubbed with a washcloth) in case the visitor was someone who'd have to be invited in and shown to the sitting-room at the back, which – although a bit damp and neglected – was always 'kept nice in case'.

If the caller was on strictly Church business, he'd be shown upstairs to Grandfather's study, lined with bookcases in which the books all had the authors' names and titles on their spines blacked out as a precaution against would-be borrowers who'd suddenly take a fancy to Dickens or Marie Corelli. His bedroom led off his study and was dark, under the yew tree's shadow, and smelled like him. Across the landing was my mother's room, where I slept too when I was small, and round a turn to the right my grandmother's, with coal and sticks piled under the bed, redolent of Pond's face cream, powder, scent, smelling salts and her town clothes in mothballs, along with a litter of underwear and stockings.

On this floor, too, was a stately lavatory, wallpapered in a perching peacock design, all intertwined feathers and branches you could contemplate for hours – which I did, legs dangling from the high wooden seat. When the chain was pulled the water tanks on the attic floor gurgled and sang. In the other attics there were apples laid out on newspaper on the floors, gently mummifying. It just wasn't a spooky house, despite the suggestive cellars, and the fact that we relied on lamps and candles. All of Hanmer did that, in any case, except for farmers who had their own generators. In the kitchen the teapot sat on the hob all day and everyone ate at different times.

There was a word that belonged to the house: 'dilapidations'. It was one of the first long words I knew, for it was repeated like a mantra. The Church charged incumbents a kind of levy for propping up its crumbling real estate and those five syllables were the key. If only Grandfather could cut down on the dilapidations there'd be a new dawn of amenity and comfort, and possibly some change left over. Leaks, dry rot, broken panes and crazy hinges (of which we had plenty) were, looked at rightly, a potential source of income. Whether he ever succeeded I don't know. Since the word went on and on, he can't have got more than a small rebate and no one ever plugged the leaks. What's certain is that we were frequently penniless and there were always embarrassments about credit. Food rationing and clothes coupons must have been a godsend since they provided a cover for our indigence. As long as austerity lasted, the vicarage could maintain its shaky claims to gentility. There was virtue in shabbiness. Grandfather had his rusty cassock, Grandmother her mothballed wardrobe and my mother had one or two pre-war outfits that just about served. Underwear was yellowed and full of holes, minus elastic. Indoors, our top layers were ragged too: matted jumpers, socks and stockings laddered and in wrinkles round the ankles, safety pins galore. Outside we could pass muster, even if my overcoat was at first too big (I would grow into it), then all at once too small, without ever for a moment being the right size.

In those years almost the whole country wore this ill-fitting uniform designed for non-combatants – serviceable colours, grating textures, tell-tale unfaded hems that had been let down, bulky tucks. Our true household craziness and indifference didn't express itself in clothes, but in more intimate kinds of squalor: for instance, nearly never washing the bits no one could see. This was almost a point of vicarage principle, a measure of our hostility to the world outside and separateness from it. Inside our clothes civilisation had lapsed. And this wasn't to do with money.

GILLIAN CLARKE
Catrin

I can remember you, child,
As I stood in a hot, white
Room at the window watching
The people and cars taking
Turn at the traffic lights.
I can remember you, our first
Fierce confrontation, the tight
Red rope of love which we both
Fought over. It was a square
Environmental blank, disinfected
Of paintings or toys. I wrote
All over the walls with my
Words, coloured the clean squares
With the wild, tender circles
Of our struggle to become
Separate. We want, we shouted,
To be two, to be ourselves.

Neither won nor lost the struggle
In the glass tank clouded with feelings
Which changed us both. Still I am fighting
You off, as you stand there
With your straight, strong, long
Brown hair and your rosy,

Defiant glare, bringing up
From the heart's pool that old rope,
Tightening about my life,
Trailing love and conflict,
As you ask may you skate
In the dark, for one more hour.

RUTH BIDGOOD
Climbing

The first time he climbed the sycamore
he called to me from his green tower
'I shall remember this all my life!'

When I was his age, staring up
into a great poplar, I knew suddenly
the same thing – that this blue sky,
these turning tilting leaves,
I would remember.

I saw branches and sunny leaves
taking me up to intoxicating heights,
wonderfully attainable. He
saw the valley from the sky, almost;
map for his journey, domain to rule.
For each, the moment climbed
high out of tick-tock time, to shine
across years, and rule the unstable dark.

PAUL GROVES
Children Playing

They do not know it, but they are
dancing towards the edge of dance,
like a drunk cartoon mouse on a table.
Adulthood is waiting to swallow play,
digest it and defecate it to enrich the soil
of its own cramped gardens, with prams,
nappies, a sleeping greenhouse dreaming of stones.

They are reproducing the enemies of childhood:
mummies and daddies, the one ironing on a bank
of green, tidying cowslip cuffs, dandelion collars,
the other relaxing in an armchair of bracken,
sucking a pipe of grass, reading *The Air News*
easily in arms which will never tire of the pages.
The land reaches out to them, offers the sweets

of innocency, and the clouds are congenial gestures.
The brooks run clear with a told-you-so, told-you-so
babble over trinket stones. How strangely
the grey pastures of commitment and responsibility
allure; how much more driving to work magnetizes
as myth than rolling over and over down
this rich hillside for ever.

PAUL HENRY
Boys

I need them, to muscle in on this silence,
to measure the softening tissue in my arms
when I carry them up to their beds,
when the old house creaks like a galleon
after a storm.

Set adrift on their dreams
their faces turn soft again.
So that one kiss carries the weight
of all we try to make light of.

EMYR HUMPHREYS
Amy Parry Visits Her Grandmother

They passed under the arch of an ancient gateway and turned to climb a narrow street with a row of houses built against the old town wall. Amy was intrigued by a yellow baker's handcart with its shafts resting in the cobbled gutter. She loitered to examine it and Esther had to urge her on. Near the top of the street the houses grew slightly larger but still stood in the shadow of the wall. The pavement narrowed. Esther knocked at a thickly painted brown door, paused for a second and then opened it. Amy stepped back reluctant to enter such a dark interior. She turned around to gaze longingly at the bright sunlight on the other side of the street. There was a dirty boy working in a tinman's repair shop next to an exposed lean-to bicycle shed that Amy expressed a sudden urge to visit.

'Is that the tinman's, Auntie? Can I go and see the tinman?'

'No, of course you can't. We've come to visit your nain. Put your hat straight, Amy.'

Immediately to the left of the door Esther had just opened, a wooden staircase wound its constricted way to another floor that was hidden in stygian darkness. Esther still stood expectantly on the narrow pavement. Amy was about to speak when she suddenly saw in the interior at a level six inches lower than the street, her grandmother standing in the kitchen doorway. Her hands folded in front of her black apron and her sallow face glimmering in the dim light as still as a painted face under the varnish of an old portrait. Her unexpectedly dark hair was parted in the middle and drawn back tightly to a severe bun on the nape of her neck. She was as quiet as a ghost. She made no move, as if unwillling to expose herself to the brightness outside her front door. She did not invite her visitors inside. Her eyes were still making a mental note of the parcels Esther was carrying: a high-priestess assessing the moral and material worth of offerings on their way to a shrine. At last a brief movement of her head implied that Esther should have compelled Amy as part of her proper training to share the load.

'Children can be very cruel.'

Her grandmother's voice was remote, monotonous and unforgiving. Amy blinked innocently. She touched Esther's skirt and looked up as if to show she expected a stout defence against any accusations about to be made. But her grandmother was talking about someone else.

'There was no need for him to go at all.'

Esther's dish hat flopped sympathetically. Amy listened to her grandmother's low voice with reverent curiosity. She could have been memorising every word she heard.

'He went against my wishes. He went because I wanted him not to go. I find it hard to forget that.'

The still unwavering stare announced that she had long experience in being called upon to try to forget and even forgive. Esther, too, had done something against her wishes. She had borne children and now she bore the wounds they chose to inflict upon her. Amy's left knee began to tremble independently as though she were forcing her legs to resist a temptation to skip and jump.

'William... Poor William...'

Esther muttered her brother's name. She was ready to weep.

'You'd better come inside,' her mother said. 'We don't want

people seeing you standing in the street outside your mother's house.'

Esther stepped forward eagerly. She was met in the confined corridor by her mother who stretched out a cold hand to open the door of the front parlour. Her formality was unobtrusive but unyielding. The room was crammed with furniture. It was as clean and as cold as a small mausoleum. The round table in the centre was covered with a chenille cloth. Every chair had a white crocheted antimacassar on the back. The black iron mantelpiece was dominated by a pair of stuffed owls under tall glass domes. Esther laid her offerings carefully on the table.

'I've brought you a gooseberry tart,' she said. 'I know you like my gooseberry tarts. We've had ever such a heavy crop in the garden this year.'

The spotless white lace curtains subdued the bright summer light. Amy's grandmother pointed silently to the sofa under the window. Esther and Amy took their seats obediently. Solemnly, she closed the door. Even this simple act seemed an assertion of power. She moved to stand by the mantelpiece, between the two owls.

' "I'm going to join the soldiers," he said. Just like that. Not a thought for his mother and what he owed her.'

'William.'

The tears accumulated in Esther's eyes. Her mother watched her as though she was about to give her permission to sob.

'Poor William.'

Esther sounded as if she was choking. Amy slid her hand along the cold surface of the horsehair sofa until her fingertips touched her aunt's clothes.

'And Lucas's brother Hugh. He is missing too. Missing believed killed. That means they're dead. Young boys dressed like soldiers. Sent away to be killed. And for what, I ask myself. For what?'

'He had to go', her mother said. 'I couldn't stop him. Your father wouldn't have stopped him either if he'd been alive. Nobody could.'

She stopped to listen to Esther weeping quietly. Amy

noticed her grandmother's goitre. It rose and fell in her neck like the only part of her rigid body allowed to move freely and express her grief. Esther's subdued sobs became melancholy music in a religious observance that obliged Amy to remain respectfully still.

' "I'm going to enlist," he said. Just like that.'

With her head turned away at an angle Amy paid close attention to her grandmother from the corner of her eyes. There was so much that was strange that she wanted to question, but she knew well enough she had been sentenced to stillness and silence for the duration of the visit.

MARY DAVIES PARNELL
A Rhondda Christmas

Particularly during the war years, Christmas seemed a bigger festival in importance, preparation and enjoyment than since and although everything – food, toys, cards, trees – was in short supply, people's spirits were high as the celebrations compensated in a small way for the deprivation and sadness of the rest of the year. No sooner was one Christmas over than the next was being looked forward to and prepared for.

Although there was a general shortage of toys for Christmas, this was not the case as far as Tump children were concerned, because in December the shop was not so much 'Philly's' or 'Jack's' as 'the Toy Shop'. During the second half of the year, my father spent increasing amounts of time in the bakehouse with his *Manual of Toy-Making* on the bench with his pieces of wood, glue and paint. Gradually the less cluttered area near the oven would be enlivened with scooters made of wood, including the wheels, painted with whatever colour paint was available; battleships – these always painted in grey with one thick black and two thin white diagonal stripes down their sides – with little bits of dowelling for guns and a mast; chunky, khaki-green camouflaged tanks; shiny, black armoured cars; and grey aeroplanes with red, white and blue circles on their wings. For younger children there were clowns, parrots or rabbits which, with a piece of wood like a pencil stuck through their bodies, would balance and roll over and over along parallel bars; and monkeys on trapezes which flung out disjointed arms and legs as they jumped and somersaulted when manipulated by squeezing two wooden shafts.

One favourite, an ingenious toy, had four or five wooden chickens on a table-tennis bat, linked by cord through small holes in the bat with a weight underneath. When the bat and consequently the weight was rotated the chickens would noisily peck imaginary food on the bat's surface. The faster the bat was rotated, the harder and faster the poor chickens' beaks would hit the surface, so that one week after Christmas most were beakless and many headless as well. Children loved these and parents tolerated the noise because it was Christmas, and longed for mid-January when they would be simply table-tennis bats and life more peaceful.

Cricket bats were simple to make, so in war-time cricket replaced football as the winter game, and for years after the war was over the Tump couldn't field a successful football team, but they were local champions at cricket.

There were rocking-horses, dolls' houses, prams, cradles and chairs, rifles and guns, skipping ropes, push-and-pull animals on wheels, carts with coloured bricks and railway engines and trucks. When ack-ack-ack or eeeeh-eeeeh-eeeeh sounds were heard around the village, it was nearly always one of father's guns or planes held aloft by a boy being a British soldier or pilot, shooting down Germans.

So during December the shop, although bare of good things to eat, had a cheerful air about it, with the colourful toys spread out for display on the shelves and in the window. Requests such as: 'A pound of flour, two candles, a Milky Lunch and two ounces of Welsh mints' were replaced by: 'Two lorries, one rocking-horse, a monkey on a stick and two warships, please'.

One year, overestimating youngsters' enthusiasm for the Navy, Dad, with my help in painting the side flashes, made too many battleships, and about a hundred of these still lay around in the bake-house in January. Although being brought up on a farm, my mother was not slow in adapting to a more commercial world and proved a good business woman. When on her bi-weekly shopping outing to Pontypridd, armed with a sample ship, she intended to approach a few war-starved stores which in normal times stocked toys to offer to sell them the warships. The first, Leslie's Stores, gladly and un-hesitatingly accepted, and my mother left with a cheque and a promise on her part not to approach any other shop. They even went so far as to send a van to fetch the ships and displayed an interest in buying any other spare toys. It seemed no sooner was the idea born than the plan was executed and Leslie's main window on Taff Street was piled high with little grey battleships with black and white side flashes. My pride knew no bounds, and to my mother's embarrassment I stood on the opposite pavement, pointing to the window and proclaiming to the passers-by: 'My daddy made those and I painted the black stripes!'

Although Christmas was well past, the ships did not last long in the store and some joy was brought to the hearts of potential British sailor boys further afield.

ALUN LLEWELYN-WILLIAMS
When I Was a Boy

All day and every day the sea sparkled, nourishing its
blueness; the sun did not portend tomorrow's storms, did
not weep for yesterday's guilt; I walked the quay in the
white morning, and questioned the masts, asking and
searching beneath the harsh gulls' tumult; and there
was my Gwennan Gorn, foal of the foam, ocean-thruster.

I lay in the bow of the boat and trailed my hands in
the water; the unbearable purity of the island's
lighthouse neared, where the fish sped and swung
below the imperturbable rock; how joyfully the sail
leapt into the blue heaven, how prettily it sank once
more into the trough of my venturesome sinews.

The green land hung in the distance like a dream
between my eyelashes, the furrows of the sea could
not count the childhood times of my journey; it was
hard, having returned, to tread the motionless earth,
to walk the clay's heaviness and to hear, now from
its cell, the mortal beating of the flesh.

It was a return without returning: those suns wore on
to their long, late sunsets; but the light in the
dusk over the bay, it is that which remains, like a miracle
snatching into that virgin tower the warm eye of the
world: just as it shone before the spies of time besieged me,
it still shines on an unfinished voyage.

ALICE THOMAS ELLIS
Growing Up in Penmaenmawr

My first teacher, Miss Roberts, a dear feathery old person, had
let me draw fairies when I should have been doing sums and I
never did get the hang of the things, so I was made to go for
private lessons to Mr Pugh, an ex-schoolteacher who lived with
his wife in a cold, clean house with a ticking clock. These
lessons were hell – as much, I imagine, for the unfortunate
Pugh as they were for me – since I was incapable even of short
division and simply couldn't see the point. He asked, one day,
as I seemed not to be concentrating, if I was frightened of him
and I explained that it was just that I'd rather be playing with
the Joneses on the clinker pile outside the laundry. Clinkers
were what was left of the coke which fed the boilers, and it has
only just occurred to me to wonder why they were dumped on
the roadside and not taken away. I don't remember the pile ever
getting any smaller.

This laundry also stood on the top road and the washing
was hung to dry in the field behind. We thought it the height of
wit to take in live shrews (which we took off the cats) to

frighten the laundry girls who all, so the local wisdom went, had perfect complexions from working in a steamy atmosphere. Jack Laundry drove the van and his wife, Jenny Laundry, made perfect chutney. Chutney was an important aspect of life in Penmaenmawr.

The Joneses – there were six of them, but the little ones didn't count much in those days – had evolved a complex and fast-moving game with a ball and the clinker heap. People were stationed at various points and heights on the clinkers, the ball went round and you took it from there. It seems perverse to have been playing on the detritus from the laundry boilers with the Snowdon range beginning behind us, but it was nearer home and our mothers could call us in for tea without having to trudge up Moelfre. The Jones children had evolved a noise – a war whoop – by which we could recognise and discover each other up on the hills. It was quite difficult to do, starting low in the throat and rising, but was effective once mastered.

I now feel nostalgic for that school by the sea. We were taught calmly and authoritatively what our teachers deemed it necessary for us to know, and often in the afternoons G.O. would tell us stories – not read out from books, but the living legends of the locality. The oral tradition was still strong then, and I can think of no better start in life for a person who is going to end up as a writer. I hated sums and the warm milk we had to drink at playtime (we used to try and shake the little bottle until the milk turned into butter – something the Celts have been doing since the dawn of history, not in bottles, natu-rally, but in skins and churns and anything which could be agitated), and Robert, who took to throwing stones at me (I still bear the scars), and being caned, which didn't happen often but was painful when it did (you were advised by your peers to spit in the hand which was going to take the punishment and lay two hairs from your head crosswise over the spit, but it didn't work), but I liked the darkening winter afternoons with the iron stove glowing and the endless stories. I think I was fortunate.

RAY MILLAND
A Wonderful Summer

I was nine years old. I knew it was going to be a wonderful summer. I knew it because the Spanish onion men were early this year. They came in March, rolling up the lanes from the estuary on foot and broken-down old bicycles. They were dressed in faded denim trousers and collarless shirts of a foreign-looking blue, rope-soled espadrilles, and big black berets, and they were shrouded, covered, in strings of onions. They were draped over their handlebars and crossbars and strung from long poles balanced on their shoulders. Always cheerful, always smiling, they would spread through the town going from house to house selling their strings of spring onions and smoked fish. Sometimes I would come home from school and a couple of them would be in the kitchen, and Mary Catherine would be gossiping and giving them tea and bread and cheese. They were Basques, you see, and between the Celtic and Basque tongues there is a connection of sorts stemming back to pre-Roman times, so it was possible to communicate, although haltingly. I would listen to their tales of Spain and Normandy and Cornwall. I think it was then I got the idea of running away to sea, although it didn't actually happen for a year or more.

My friend and constant conspirator, Donald Hope, and I used to spend hours dreaming it and planning it, sitting high in an oak tree in the woods at the top of the hill. It seemed easy to us, because Donald's father was manager of the ship-breaking yard of Thomas W. Ward and Company, which was situated at Briton Ferry some five miles away at the mouth of the river. Weary old coasters and sad and rusty freighters were there waiting for the torch. And there would always be one old tramp steamer tied up, loading scrap. I think I was ten years old when Donald sneaked up to me one day in school and said there was a freighter in the yard, unloading hides, that would probably sail again the following Saturday. This was it! High tide would not be until midday, so if we met at four A.M. Saturday morning and walked fast, we could easily be there by six A.M. And that's what we did. We fortified ourselves with paper bags filled with bread and jam and seed cake and a couple of bottles of small beer and set off. We got to the yard and found the boat without any trouble. It was tied up at the small commercial wharf next to the yard, and on the stern I saw painted its port of registry. Santos! All my geography came alive. I saw trees with monkeys, unlimited bananas, pampas grass, and the wonderful smell of coffee bags.

The ship was strangely silent and deserted. So we scrambled aboard quite undetected and saw that the hatch covers were off. We picked the one amidships and quickly climbed down the iron ladder and went to the farthest and darkest corner, where we found a pile of sacking and old canvas. There we made our little nest, sat and waited, and had some small beer. And sat and waited. There was never a sound. It was Saturday. We were tired from the long walk, so we decided to sleep for a while. It must have been four or five hours later that I was awakened by footsteps on the iron deck above. I quietly climbed the iron ladder and peeked over the coaming; there were three men standing about thirty feet away from me looking forward, and I heard one of them say, 'We'll get those two donkey engines off first thing Monday morning, they're worth saving, and there's a couple of generators in the engine room worth a pound or two. By the end of the week we can start cutting her up.'

I went back down and walked slowly over to Donald and told him what I'd heard. I said we'd better go home. He looked at me wide-eyed for a moment and started to cry. It embarrassed me, so I started to pat him. I didn't know what else to do. I said, 'It's no use carrying on like that. Tell them back at your house that we walked to Baglan Sands to look for mussels. And the tide was in so we couldn't get any. They'll never know the difference.' With that, he started bawling more than ever. I whispered at him as loud as I dared, 'Shut up, those men will hear you!'

Then he said, 'I forgot to tell you. I left my mother a note!'

Now this properly enraged me. 'You *mochen*, you *dwlben!* Now you've done it! My dada'll kill me!'

I sat down chastened. How was I to fiddle my way out of this situation? No way. Just would have to go home and face the music. There'd be plenty of it, and it wouldn't be 'The Dream of Gerontius.'

We sat there and ate the rest of the seed cake and drank the small beer, waiting for the men to leave and for the boat to be deserted and the yard empty again. It was almost four o'clock before we could start back, only this time the journey didn't seem so far. Our homes were approaching much too quickly. There was a small farmhouse set back from the road, its large front garden a mass of red-currant bushes, so we crawled in among them and sat there morosely, more or less trying to stave off the moment of truth. We started to eat the red currants; they were delicious, so we ate a bellyful. Then there was nothing else to do, so we set out on the last mile. When we got to the fork in the road we separated, he to his house, I to mine. Today, when I think of it, I always giggle. He looked just like Stan Laurel having to do something that Ollie had forced him into.

When I got to my house I knocked on the door, something I had never done before. It was opened by Williams the Police. 'Oh, come home, have you? Well, your father wants to see you, Reggie *bach*.' And with that he left.

I looked at my father, and *he* looked at *me* and then pointed to the stairs. As I went up I saw him reach for the wall of the passage on which hung some polished brass bed-warmers on long wooden handles, some horse brasses, and a couple of toasting forks about four feet long. His hand came away with a toasting fork. Up in the bedroom I gave a sterling performance. My bawling had everything – pathos, agony, total abandonment, and just the right touch of Sydney Carton. I even managed to throw up a little, and at that moment in charged my mother and Mary Catherine. 'What are you doing to this poor child? What sort of father are you?'

And from Mary Catherine – 'You ought to be ashamed of yourself, you've even bent the toasting fork. Oh, and look! He's bleeding from the mouth! Oh, what a proper beast you are!'

My father looked at them completely distraught, and I saw

tears in his eyes; his emotions were always so close to the surface. Then he stumbled out. Mary Catherine went to the washstand, wet a towel, and came back to wash the blood from my mouth. I told them not to worry, that it was only red currants. With that my mother belted me in the ear, and they both left.

I lay there sniffling for a while and then undressed and climbed into bed. No use expecting supper this night, which was all right with me. Couldn't eat anyway.

DERYN REES-JONES
Half-term

> She speaks to me in a language that is no language.
> But I understand it... Speaking her old, old language
> of words that are not words.
>
> Jean Rhys

November – a week in Aberystwyth with an aunt
and words I couldn't understand – iawn iawn iawn

bechod iawn – until shooed upstairs
to the saying of prayers and a great brass bed.

Much later, to the click of a clock
and the soft night noise of street and sea,

my dreams came sleepily
like sloppy slippered feet as Nesta

in a long white dress moved spookily,
hiding her nakedness, the terrible lopsidedness

of only one breast. She clambered in
beside me – flat chested in my boneful body

linen cocooned, almost awake, I
rested my head. That gap was delicate

as Summer flowers, and pressed like sealing wax
on letters from the past. And I remember that

she sang to me – oh dee oh doh – as out
over a ridge of anonymous roofs. Winter

serrated an emptiness of sky
to a shiver of cold stars. Snow.

GLENDA BEAGAN
Heather and Gavin

It was like a young shark. Lithe, streamlined, with a fierce face.

'What is it?' Gavin asked.

'I dunno,' said Heather.

'It'll die if it stays there.'

'No it won't, stupid. When the tide comes in it'll swim off won't it?'

'But it's going to get worn out. It's going to hurt itself. Look.'

And she looked. Despite herself. Wrinkling up her face as the creature lashed and fought against the rock. The air was full of the sharp crack of its tail and arching back. She wanted to close her eyes. Get away from here. The shallow water trapping it in the pool, the crack between the layered slabs, seemed to sting to burn with its fury.

'We'll have to save it.'

'How?'

She heard the sound of her voice become hard, contemptuous. She heard the sneer in it. Why did she have to put up with him all the time? Drag him around everywhere? This place was boring now. She didn't see why she had to come here at all. Why wouldn't they let her go and stay with Claire and Miriam in Guildford?

'I'm going to try and save it.'

'It'll bite you. You'll fall in or something and they'll blame me. Why can't you leave things alone?'

Gavin wasn't listening. He was crouched down on the rocks staring hard at the fish thing as it writhed.

'I just wish we could tell it to wait. To be quiet and wait for the tide.'

'That's what I said. But it's stupid isn't it? It's like you. It hasn't got a brain.'

Again he ignored her. It was difficult to get a foothold near enough, among all the weed. Bladderwrack with its blobs for popping. Slithery thongweed. Where could he grip? By the tail? It was big though, wasn't it? And slippery. And it wasn't in the best of tempers.

He'd thought it out. You could tell. Heather wanted to walk away. Leave him. But she couldn't. There he was, like a Red Indian or something, crouched there. Oblivious of her. Oblivious of everything. And she knew, deep down inside, that Gavin was simply better than she was. He was different, yes, but it was more than that. More than their mother would allow. She always said they were chalk and cheese and made a joke about it. But it wasn't funny. At all.

Around them the sea, the sky, the sounds of the estuary. Oystercatchers making their tinny cry. Was it a sad cry? Was it happy? She couldn't decide. Anymore than she could decide whether the lighthouse on its thin, and from here almost invis-ible, island was something she loved or hated. She turned back to him. She wanted to say something spiteful. But she couldn't. In a horrible way, she knew Gavin was good. Simply good. And knowing that made her feel small and mean inside.

'I've got him.'

Gavin's shout, Gavin's running, was everywhere. The whole place, the rocks, the clouds, the air, was full of Gavin. And the fish thing, that was Gavin too, as he went hurtling off over the glittering wet stones of the promontory, with it wriggling, fight-ing in his grip. Almost slipping, almost flat on his face, but catching himself as he started to fall, swivelling back upright, then on again, until, just at the point where the stones filtered out, and the deep channel of the river, narrow and deep, a dark green, almost black, reached the sea, he stopped, raising both hands with the great slippery fish thing between them, and flung. And as the fish hit the water there was a sound like a door slamming, or a gun going off. A sideways, steady fling, with hardly a splash, so the fish joined the current at just the right angle, in just the right place.

'You should've seen it,' he said, catching up with her, breathless, as she picked her way back. 'It was brilliant. Just like it was flying.' And it wasn't as if he was showing off or anything. He wasn't like that. He just wanted to share it with her. 'Great,' she said, struggling. And then he was off again, running back to the house, past the upturned boats pulled high up on the sandy bit.

CATHERINE MERRIMAN
The Milky Way

'This can't take long,' said Susan, pulling the heavy latched door of the cottage to behind her. 'I've got to ring your father before ten.'

'Just along here,' said Jamie's voice, disembodied in the darkness, somewhere the other side of the garden lawn. 'It has to be away from the lights.'

Susan sighed, and with an edge of humour she didn't actually feel, said, 'This had better be worth it.' She stepped, reluctantly, onto the dewy grass. Her canvas shoes were going to get soaked. Where was her son taking her? Ugh, she could feel a chilly dampness already. At the bottom of the lawn she heard a familiar rattle and creak. Oh God, he was through into the field. Groping for the swinging garden gate she called irritably, 'Where are we going, Jamie?' Then made an effort – this was meant to be a surprise for her, a treat, even – and called again, more lightly, 'Jamie?'

'Here.' There was still eagerness in her son's voice. She felt a pang of shame, and then gratitude, for the uncrushable optimism and tolerance of her child. She sighed again, Why were his surprises so wearisome? Why did they oppress her so? And what would it be, this time? Probably an animal. That's why he wouldn't use the handlamp. A hedgehog? Toad? Glow-worm? Something of wonder to a thirteen-year-old. She could hear herself saying, fervently, 'Oh, marvellous, Jamie.' Feeling dutiful, for expressing wonder, and inadequate, for having to pretend it.

In the darkness she stumbled over a tussock of long scratchy grass. 'Oh hell,' she said, forgetting good intentions and thinking of her tights, 'Jamie! Put the bloody torch on.'

'You don't need it,' said Jamie's voice, close beside her. 'This'll do. Stand still.'

Susan stood still. The lights of the house had disappeared behind the garden hedge. She could only just make out Jamie, a darker, denser shape in the blackness.

'Well?' she said.

'Look up.'

She looked up vaguely. 'What?'

'Oh Mummy.' Jamie sounded exasperated. 'Look.'

She stared up and felt, as a telescopic process, her vision stretch outwards into the night. Her eyes refocused. Millions of stars, from brilliant cats'-eyes to diamond dust, arched in a frozen swirl across the night sky.

'It's the Milky Way,' she said. Of course, she had seen it before, often. But still. Sincerely she said, 'Beautiful, isn't it.' Her son had brought her out to see the stars. How touching. She wondered how long she should stay, marvelling at them, to show her appreciation.

'Now,' Jamie said, sounding not awestruck, but business-like. 'Come closer.'

Oh dear, there was more. Susan twisted her wrist, before realizing she wouldn't be able to read her watch. Suppressing a tick of impatience – it must be nearly ten – she moved closer.

'Right,' Jamie said. He was so near she could hear the catarrhal rasp of his breathing. He's as tall as I am, she thought. He seems even taller in the dark. But he still breathes like a child. His elbow brushed against her arm, as he did something with the torch.

'OK,' he said. 'Now, get really close, and follow the line of the beam. Keep behind it, or you'll be dazzled.'

She heard a click. From his chest a powerful beam shot upwards to the sky.

'Gracious!' she said. For a second the beam looked like a heart-light, emerging from her son; leading straight up to the stars. She recollected herself, and gave a short laugh. 'You must have bought a new battery.'

'Yup,' said Jamie, sounding smug. 'You need a powerful torch for this.'

He swung the beam from horizon to horizon like a searchlight, then steadied it.

'Put your head close to mine.' He waited for Susan to obey him. 'Right, now, that group of stars there. Can you see them?'

Susan followed the line of the beam upwards. How impressive. She could see exactly the stars he meant, just outside the dense swirl of the Milky Way. The beam appeared to bathe them in pale light. She nodded and said, 'Yes, I see them.'

'That's Orion.'

'Is it?' she said. 'How clever of you. And what a good way of pointing them out. It's like using a ruler on a blackboard.'

She pulled back. 'Where on earth did you learn to do this?'

'On the geography field trip,' Jamie said. 'Mr Haines is mad about stars.' He moved the beam a fraction away.

'There, that's the Pleiades... see? And that bright star there... Aldebaran. In Taurus.'

'Where's... um...' It took Susan a second to think of a heavenly body, '...the Plough?'

'Ah,' said Jamie. 'That's the other side of the Milky Way.' He swung the beam across the sky and resettled it. 'There... see?'

JEREMY BROOKS
Love in Llandudno

Kathy entered my life quietly, like a ship, with its engines cut, sliding silently into its berth across a still mirror of water. After our first brief meeting on the threshold of the school, I continued to see her more and more frequently about the streets, the playing-fields, the beaches, and the hills. It was Gregory, of course, who discovered and passed on her name; and by shadowing her, one day after school, hazardously through the streets from the Library down to Craig-y-don, I had found out where she lived. Gradually, she began to enter my waking dreams; became the audience, breathless with suspense, for whom I climbed the unclimbable mountains or broke the unbreakable stallions. So familiar did her presence become to me in these dreams, that it seemed only natural that in my active life our paths should cross so frequently.

In fact, our brief meetings became so regular as to be beyond the scope of coincidence; one broiling May afternoon – a Sunday – I stumbled across her, with two other girls, picnicking on the summit of Conway Mountain; the next evening, after school, when I was cycling by myself round to Rhos-on-Sea by way of Llangwstenin, she suddenly appeared on the road in front of me, walking slowly, but apparently puffed with running; and at Gogarth Abbey, two evenings later, where I was waiting for Jones, who had some errand to complete for his mother, I spotted Kathy walking lazily along the Marine Drive above me, seemingly intent on her own thoughts. Jones had still not arrived, and I was passing the time by throwing stones at the wheeling seagulls below me, when Kathy passed again on her way back. This time she saw me, and waved; and hesitated, so that for a moment I thought she was going to clamber over the wall and climb down the rocks to join me.

Now when our paths crossed we would exchange brief greetings, and often pause for a moment, looking at each other undecidedly, until one or the other of us made a sudden gesture of retreat. On one occasion, Dora Maguire held me talking, on some pretext, as she waited at the gate of the school long after the majority had left; and I, anxious to get away, had just impatiently cut short the conversation and turned to leave when I saw Kathy emerging from the girls' cloakroom, and realized that it was for her Dora had been waiting. But it was by then too late for me to stay, my excuses and goodbyes to Dora had been made, so there was nothing for me to do but cycle as quickly as possible away, knowing that by my obtuseness (for it had at last dawned on me that Dora had thought to effect a meeting between us thus) and impatience I had forfeited the chance of a perfectly simple, authentically accidental, introduction.

But, as it turned out, such an introduction became unnecessary. Shortly afterwards, as I was cycling down the Conway Road on my way home after walking through the town and back again with Jones – an after-school ritual which had the same social importance as riding down Rotten Row or along the Promenade at Longchamps – I came across Kathy, leaning over her bicycle and fiddling with the chain, which had slipped off the rear cog. Without any sense of surprise, and only the very faintest quickening of the heart, I pulled up beside her and asked if I could help. She looked up quickly as I spoke, and said quietly: 'Oh, hello! No, I think I've fixed it now, thanks!' She gave a turn to the wheel, and I heard the chain click back into place. She seemed to have managed the whole operation without getting a trace of grease on her hands, but nevertheless went busily through the ritual of finding a clean white rag in her saddlebag, wiping her hands, folding the rag, and returning it neatly to its pocket. Then she straightened up, smiled shyly, and began to mount her bicycle. She had a frail gold chain round her left wrist.

It was a quietly miraculous event. Her tone, as she said 'Oh, hello!' had been familiar, unsurprised, as if she had only left my company a moment before; and so natural did it seem to me to be with her, that I was aware of nothing unusual in the ease with which we cycled off together towards the Links Hotel. When two eight-year-old urchins called from the pavement: 'Sweethearts! Sweethearts!' as we cycled past, we exchanged smiles of compassion for them; and I was pleased to think that the thing was accomplished and obvious already, without my having had to expose myself to the dangers of taking action.

PETER FINCH

The Tattoo

At the ferro-concrete bike sheds
I pass a love-note to Veronica.
I wear long trousers and brylcream now
but her only interest is proven prowess.
I tattoo her name on my arm in Quink
with a penknife and show her.
She is unimpressed.
She goes out with a big ted from the fifth
who pisses over bog doors when you're in there.
He wears knuckle-dusters and can make a noise like a fart
with his armpit. Everyone is scared.
At break the Head tells me
that only criminals and soldiers sport tattoos
and sends me home to remove it.
My mother refuses. There is a dispute.
Magnificently my photograph
appears in the paper. Schoolboy Banned.
Our family are resolute.

Its over when by mistake
I wash a week later
and the whole thing goes.
I return to school a hero
where after assembly Veronica smiles
and the big ted breaks my nose.

PHIL CARRADICE
Jenny

Jenny was my first love.

I was barely fourteen years old and – oh yes – I know what the cynics would say – it was mere infatuation, the calf-like, moon-struck burgeoning of early adolescence. But for those few, fabulous months it was, to me, real and glorious and vital. I had never felt such exquisite pain before and, to be frank, I don't think I've ever experienced quite the same sensation again.

The first thing I knew about it was in the school changing-rooms one fine Saturday morning in April. We had just played our last match of the season, beating our arch rivals in a fast and hard-fought game. I was standing in front of my locker, body tingling with the heat from the showers, tentatively fingering a bruise on my left temple.

'Hey, what's this I hear about you and Jenny Stephens?' called Pete across the steam-filled room.

There was a shout of laughter from the other boys and, from around the corner of the coat racks, somebody's wet towel flicked out at my bare backside.

'What the hell are you on about?' I countered, flinging a discarded rugby boot in the general direction of my assailant.

'It's all over the school,' Pete yelled. 'She fancies you something rotten. Says she wants to go out with you. God knows why. Spotty bloody Muldoon!'

Ignoring the laughter, I frowned at my mate Bob and busied myself with packing away my muddy kit. The colour had rushed to my face but there was a strange, warm glow in my stomach.

'First thing I've heard about it,' I called over my shoulder. 'Wouldn't go out with her, anyway. She's a bloody dog.'

When Bob and I left the changing rooms a little later a small blond boy I recognised as a first-former was sitting on the bottom step. He jumped up quickly when he saw us and thrust a crumpled note into my hands.

'From Jenny,' he said, inclining his head towards the girls' hockey pitch. 'No answer needed.'

I watched his thin legs hurry him away across the play-ground. Bob nudged me and motioned at the slip of paper. 'Better read it,' he said. 'Might be something important.'

I was embarrassed, reluctant to open the letter. I could see the interest on Bob's face and knew that if I was too secretive all sorts of rumours would be around school in a matter of hours. So, resignedly, I ripped open the paper.

'Do you fancy a game of tennis this afternoon?' the note read. 'If you do, meet me on the old course at 2.30. Love Jenny.'

I shrugged.

'See? Nothing to it. She wants a game of tennis, that's all.'

Bob leered at me.

'Really? Well, if she does, it's not for your backhand drive, that's for sure. You're bloody naive, son!'

We sauntered off to the bus-stop. I was pleased, elated even. Girls hadn't bothered me much up till now. To tell the truth, they'd never seemed interested in me, always preferring hand-some swaggerers like Bob and Pete. So now, to find Jenny – decidedly one of the more desirable elements in the school – actually interested in me? Well, it was too much.

LEONORA BRITO

Lesley-Ann

Her mother was wearing a blue smock over her black skirt, there was a safety-pin in the zip of the skirt, because it would-n't do up anymore. The girl knew her mother was expecting. No-one had mentioned it to her, Lesley-Ann, specifically. They would be too embarrassed: her mother and father never talked about things like that – her mother wouldn't even say the word 'bra' – she wrote it down when she sent Lesley-Ann to the shops. In real writing, she wrote: 'One pr. of brassiers' and, in brackets, '(36c)'. When Lesley-Ann had been about eleven (she was thirteen now) the girl behind the counter hadn't read the note properly and had sent Lesley-Ann home with a pair of boy's braces. Her mother had turned the braces over and over in her hands, fingering the silver clip-on things as if she couldn't make out what they were. 'I don't know how they come to –' she had said, and stopped. 'They're –'. She had stopped again, annoyed and embarrassed. So when Lesley-Ann came downstairs one morning and saw her mother standing at the sink in a smock she thought: oh, she must be expecting, but she hadn't said anything.

Her mother reached into the sink and picked up the fish slice. She ran it under the tap and wiped it clean with a cloth. More work! Then she gave the chips in the pan a shake. Lesley-Ann's mother shook the long handle on the frying pan as if it was someone's throat. A loud sizzling noise filled the small kitchen. Her mother looked over her shoulder at Lesley-Ann. 'Open that tin of beans for me,' she said. 'See if you can do that.'

Her father came home from work at six o'clock and they had their dinner then. They sat in their living-room and ate from the trays in their laps. The television was on in the corner. Their heads went down, then up, as the pictures flickered from light to dark on the screen. They were watching the news. Usually no-one spoke until after the news was finished. Lesley-Ann ate her sausages, beans and chips, and looked at the television-set. In black and white, she thought, the news is. But it was grey really, when you looked at it – when you put your eyes up close to the set, you saw a swarm of grey things crawling behind the glass like millions of amoebas.

She thought back to the morning, when she had looked out of the window of the bus. The bus had gone past the pub, just a little way down from where the dog was, and she had looked out and seen these three people, getting into a car: two bandsmen in bright red jackets, and a girl, standing between them. The girl was wearing a mohair dress. The dress was red, but not bright red, like the men's jackets.

Lesley-Ann looked at her parents. It was on the tip of her tongue to tell them. She looked at her mother. Her mother was in a better mood, now that all the cooking was over. Lesley-Ann took a deep breath: 'Can people get married on a Friday,' she asked, 'or not?'

Her voice came out sounding like a ten-year old's. It was the type of question a ten-year old would ask, and she was given an answer straightaway. Quick as a quiz contestant her mother said 'yes, of course they can. Think there's only one day of the week people can get married on?' She looked towards Lesley-Ann's father and laughed. Her father nodded and said yes. 'Any day of the week, bar a Monday', he screwed up his face, 'and a Sunday.'

Lesley-Ann said 'oh', and thought a little bit. 'They must have been going to a wedding then,' she said out loud, as if she was talking to herself. And when her mother asked her, 'who?' Lesley-Ann said: 'These three people I saw this morning'; and she told them about the girl and the two bandsmen. 'They were all dressed up,' she told them, 'in red uniforms, the men were...'.

'I wonder if that's that Kelvin.' Her mother turned to her father. He looked at her and said: 'What Kelvin?'

'You know the one I mean.' Lesley-Ann's mother knit her eyebrows together, thinking. 'You know –' she nudged his arm and said, 'You do!' He remembered then. His face cleared all of a sudden and he slapped his hand on the knee of his dungarees.

'Oh yeah,' he said, looking up at the light-bulb, 'him!'

Only a few words. Lesley-Ann stood at the stainless steel sink and dipped the plates into the hot soapy water, one by one. Her mother and father used only a few words between them, she thought, lifting a plate from out of the water and examining the bubbles minutely – but those few words spoke volumes. Her eyes focused on the bubbles' shimmering plaid of pinks and greens and violets, before she dipped the plate back into the water and out again, hardly touching it. Just holding with four fingers, two on either side of the scalloped edges, which was how the woman did the dishes on the advert. She put the plate in the rack to drain, and went on with her thinking, trawling beneath the surface of the water for things to lift up to the light and stack. People spoke words from their mouths, she reasoned slowly. They sent them out into space, which was volume, which was air – cubic metres of air into which people sent out words – only a few at a time. And other people who were on the same wavelength picked up those words and amplified them, sending out words of their own. Which became a conversation, loud and clear.

BERNICE RUBENS
A Festive Meal

Mr Thomas arrived at one o'clock, bringing with him his chair, a whole week's sweet ration, and one egg. He was dressed in a suit, probably the only suit he had ever possessed, for it had an old-fashioned look with its wide lapels and even wider turn-ups. The cloth, though shiny now, looked of good stock, and I had the feeling that he had worn it at his wedding, and had I been able to look in his pockets, I might have found traces of faded confetti. He hung on to his chair, holding it close to his body like a shield.

'Put it down by the table, Mr Thomas,' my dad said. They'd known each other all the years they'd been in the terrace, but in all that time, neither man, nor their women for that matter, had offered their Christian names. It was the same with our lodgers, even though they shared our bathroom. Mr Travers and Mr Philips they were. As paying guests they were entitled to their surnames. My mam insisted on it. Christian names would only do for lodgers.

We had sweet sherry before dinner. There was the half a bottle over from last Christmas, together with half a bottle of brandy which Auntie Annie had brought two Christmases ago. Mr Travers and Mr Philips had brought an illegal bottle of wine each, and their gifts were accepted with the silence granted to bootleggers. The parlour had not been used since the Christmas of last year and the paper loops and streamers still hung from the ceiling, heavy with accumulated dust.

The guests had all arrived promptly. My mam wanted our dinner over by three o'clock so that we could all listen to King

George and his Christmas message. I used to feel sorry for him. All over England and Wales people would switch on the wireless at three o'clock and only to listen to his stammering. Would the poor bugger make it to the end of the sentence? Men who never gambled in their lives would lay a Christmas bet on the poor King's articulation. Whatever he had to say went unheeded and unheard. All that mattered was whether he managed or not to spill it out at all. Cruel it was, I thought, and not like my mam and dad at all. Especially, my dad. He was a shy man, and gentle. He didn't say very much but I know he had deep feelings. He was always so kind to everybody. Except to poor King George on Christmas Day. On every other day of the year he thought the King was special, there by divine right, he used to say. I suppose he needed to find some flaw in that perfection, and the stammer would do for the feet of clay. We sat around sipping our sherry and nobody said anything, as if sherry-sipping was a full-time occupation. I noticed that Mr Philips' glass was empty but he went on sipping anyway so as not to look out of things. My dad was taking his time. He didn't like sherry very much, not so much for the taste of it but for its class, which he equated with a more affluent setting than our own. He saw it in a decanter, with cigars and *The Times* newspaper within its reach. He hated the sherry classes and all that they stood for. But my mam sipped it with relish and wished that every day was Christmas.

We settled ourselves around the table, and my mam brought in the big tureen of soup. Tomato it was, our favourite. Tinned soup, and the very best. Gold it was in those days. Canned food wasn't rationed but it was in short supply. But the corner grocer had a soft spot for my mam. Or that's what my mam thought. But I knew otherwise, because it was me he had the soft spot for. 'Send your girl in,' he'd say to my mam. 'I'll have something for her.' And then my mam would send me to the corner and in exchange for a tickle in the nether folds of my pleated gym slip, I would be rewarded with a tin of couponless nourishment. I didn't mind really. Over the weeks my pleats became shamelessly frayed, but it was a small price to pay for the heaven of tomato soup.

My mam ladled it out with reverence. She sprinkled a little parsley on the top, her sole contribution, apart from the tin-opener, to the first course. It looked pretty, the green and the red, and I viewed my portion for a while because it seemed a pity to disturb the pattern.

'Get that soup down you now,' my mam said, 'before it gets stone cold.'

I was the last to finish the soup and I felt all their eyes on me, and my soup spoon began to tremble with embarrassment. But I did not hurry myself. When I look back on it now, I suppose I must have been doing my bit to postpone the turkey and the carving knife, though at the time I was conscious of no troubling thought in that direction. I felt them waiting for me around the table. In time I finished the soup, but a scattering of parsley still lay around the bowl and rim of the plate, irretrievable by spoon. Only a finger could gather them. This I used while my mam gasped, 'Manners!' and my dad smiled at the lodgers and Mr Thomas to prevent their censure. I gathered the bowls into a pile and took them to the kitchen. 'Manners,' I heard my mam say again and I waited for its echo to fade before I returned to the parlour.

LEWIS JONES
Len's First Day

Len's exhaustion vanished with the knowledge that the interminable trudge was over and that he was now in his father's working place. He started to pull off his coat, when Jim interrupted him testily. Not by there, boy bach. Shift under those timbers, where you will be safe.'

Len did as he was told, and putting his box and jack carefully at the foot of a strong-looking prop, he pulled off his coat and shirt. He paused at this until he saw Jim pull off the singlet next his skin; then he did the same, and immediately felt the air beat more cool and pleasantly upon his naked chest.

'Duw, that be nice, dad,' he said, revived by the contact.

'Huh,' grunted Jim. 'Take the tools off the bar. Here be the key.'

Len did so, then, with a shovel in his hands, he followed his father on hands and knees through the coal-face. The glistening coal, reflecting the gleam from the two lamps, fascinated Len. He watched Jim crawl, practically on his stomach, up the long stretch of the coal face until only the dim light of his lamp was visible. Scared to be left alone, the lad followed, only to be gruffly ordered back.

'You keep by that empty tram and don't move till I tell you.'

Len turned back and for the first time gave conscious thought to the tram. It stood end on to the clear-cut roof, or 'rippings,' which had to be blown down as the coal-face advanced, so that the tram could follow the coal.

A deep feeling of loneliness enveloped Len as he wondered what would happen if his father were not near and he were left entirely on his own. All round him he could hear little move-ments, as if the place were alive. He had an uncanny feeling that the roof was moving, and each creak of the timbers, as they unwillingly took the weight of the settling strata, sent a quiver through his body. He had yet to learn that the pit had a life of its own, that it was never still or silent, but was always moving and moaning in response to the atmosphere and pressure.

Suddenly he felt a burning sensation on his stomach. His hand flashed to the spot automatically, his fingers clutched some object and tore it away, and opening his hand he saw a huge red insect with innumerable hairy legs and hard, shiny wings. Although crushed in his convulsive grip, the ghastly legs still beat the air, and looking down at his belly, he saw a thin stream of blood running down it where the cockroach had gripped the flesh and torn it away. A sick giddiness swept over the lad for a moment, while the perspiration burst from every pore in his body, lathering it in a mixture of coal-dust and moisture, but before he could recover from the shock he heard his father crawling back. This proof that he was not alone encouraged the lad and he was smiling when Big Jim emerged on the roadway.

'We will work in the right hand cut to-day, Len bach,' he said, 'so that we can free the whole face for to-morrow.'

Len did not understand the technique underlying the remark, but he asked with assumed indifference, 'What be I to do, dad?'

Jim replied: 'You will come up the cut with me and throw the coal back towards the tram.'

The lad obeyed, and followed his father, and for hours he worked on his knees with the back of his head rubbing against the roof. He began mentally counting each shovelful of coal his father cut and which he had to throw back to the tram. His arms grew heavy as lead, cramp caught him in his bent legs, and his back felt as though it were broken. The coal-dust that filled the air got into his nose and eyes. It made him sneeze and blink and, working into the sweat-opened pores of his body, set up an intolerable irritation. He felt it impossible to lift another shovelful of the coal he now detested, but somehow he kept on, until at last his father said:

'That will do for now. Let's go back and get a bit of tommy.'

The lad dragged his weary, painful limbs back into the road-way, where he stretched himself full length in the dust. He saw his heart pumping against the bones of his naked chest, and felt pins and needles run through his flesh in spasms of excruciating agony.

Big Jim, sensing what was happening, urged him to his feet. 'Come on. Get up before you go stiff.'

With infinite care Len dragged his limbs together and slowly rose to his feet. He opened his food box and sat down. The bread-and-butter looked dirty and un-appetising, but the water in his jack was like nectar. Jim stopped him before he had emptied the tin of its contents. 'Don't do that again or you will get cramp in your belly. Get on with your food.'

The lad tried to obey, but the hundreds of savage-looking cockroaches that buzzed and fussed around turned his stomach, while the dust he had already swallowed curdled in his inside.

After a while Big Jim rose and made his way back up the face, telling Len: 'You stop there till I shout for you. A bit of a whiff 'on't do you any harm now.'

During the rest the lad slowly recovered from his exhaustion. The black dust under his body seemed softer and more sweet to him then than even the green grass on his beloved mountain, and his mind wandered to the end of the shift. Before his eyes floated a picture of the envious glances of his schoolmates when they saw him striding, black-faced, down the hill in his working clothes. He saw the glad look in his mother's eyes as he walked into the little kitchen, having finished his day's work. Already he began to count the pocket-money he would have in a fortnight's time, and speculated how best to spend it.

Part Three

Sir! Don' keep askin' me
wha' we should do,
yew're the bloody teacher!

EWART ALEXANDER
The First Memorable Happening

I suppose the first memorable happening, excepting that great ride on a fire engine, was being carried to school by Uncle Hayden. I'd told my mother at about four years of age, in summer it must have been because Hayden appeared on the sky-line like a young beech, that I wasn't going to school. What trauma gave rise to this attitude of mine isn't clear, but feeling helpless on Hayden's shoulder is still like the rub of a familiar garment. He played rugby and was strong and big and I must have looked and sounded like a piglet going reluctantly to market. Some years later, Hayden gave me my first real rugby jersey and it was in this that I scored my first try in a proper game. We are good friends now. So to school then.

Creepy crawly Miss James, who had favourites and who showed this in the gifts at Christmas, was a tall old bitch who let you play in the sand in exchange for a strong feeling of guilt, and sometimes let you sit on the rocking-horse in exchange for behaviour well above and beyond the mortal, unless of course, you were a favourite of hers. No wonder I didn't want to spend time in her company, but then I was made to feel very wrong and now I know I was very right. Miss Jenkins kept me away from Teddy who had lice. She taught us in a class-room like a lecture room so that descending those steps to the blackboard was like dropping into a pit. She was a bit of a Bible-puncher, so, not only having to contend with insidious glidings of Miss James, God was ever ready to trip me in the aisles. Then two years later I had terrible trouble with fractions, but eventually Miss Daniels came up to the back and showed me the secret. The following year I met my first scholar though at the time I wouldn't have recognised him even if I'd been told. Walter Watkins, most of all in those days, got me through the eleven-plus and it's almost a cliche to say nice things about someone or other, but this man has said, over the years, the most mean-ingful things to me. He has also demonstrated what generosity means. I would hope that everyone, sometime or other, had someone at hand to show a poem just because it's an enjoyable experience to be shared. Nothing else matters for those moments than someone's poem is being read and maybe felt, and for a boy, this can show that there are things other than guilty sand.

EVELYN WAUGH
Llanabba School

As the bell stopped ringing Dr Fagan swept into the hall, the robes of a Doctor of Philosophy swelling and billowing about him. He wore an orchid in his buttonhole.

'Good morning, gentlemen,' he said.

'Good morning, sir,' chorused the boys.

The Doctor advanced to the table at the end of the room, picked up a Bible, and opening it at random, read a chapter of blood-curdling military history without any evident relish. From that he plunged into the Lord's Prayer, which the boys took up in a quiet chatter. Prendergast's voice led them in tones that testified to his ecclesiastical past.

Then the Doctor glanced at a sheet of notes he held in his hand. 'Boys,' he said, 'I have some announcements to make. The Fagan cross-country running challenge cup will not be competed for this year on account of the floods.'

'I expect the old boy has popped it,' said Grimes in Paul's ear.

'Nor will the Llanabba Essay Prize.'

'On account of the floods,' said Grimes.

'I have received my account for the telephone,' proceeded Dr Fagan, 'and I find that during the past quarter there have been no less than twenty-three trunk calls to London, none of which was sent by me or by members of my family. I look to the prefects to stop this, unless of course they are themselves responsible, in which case I must urge them in my own interests to make use of the village post-office, to which they have access.

'I think that is everything, isn't it, Mr Prendergast?'

'*Cigars*,' said Mr Prendergast in a stage whisper.

'Ah yes, cigars. Boys, I have been deeply distressed to learn that several cigar ends have been found – where have they been found?'

'*Boiler-room.*'

'In the boiler-room. I regard this as reprehensible. What boy has been smoking cigars in the boiler-room?'

There was a prolonged silence, during which the Doctor's eye travelled down the line of boys.

'I will give the culprit until luncheon to give himself up. If I do not hear from him by then the whole school will be heavily punished.'

'Damn!' said Grimes. 'I gave those cigars to Clutterbuck. I hope the little beast has the sense to keep quiet.'

'Go to your classes,' said the Doctor.

The boys filed out.

'I should think, by the look of them, they were exceedingly cheap cigars,' added Mr Prendergast sadly. 'They were a pale yellow colour.'

'That makes it worse,' said the Doctor. 'To think of any boy under my charge smoking pale yellow cigars in a boiler-room! It is *not* a gentlemanly fault.'

The masters went upstairs.

'That's your little mob in there,' said Grimes, 'you let them out at eleven.'

'But what am I to teach them?' said Paul in sudden panic.

'Oh, I shouldn't try to *teach* them anything, not just yet, anyway. Just keep them quiet.'

'Now that's a thing I've never learned to do,' sighed Mr Prendergast.

Paul watched him amble into his classroom at the end of the passage, where a burst of applause greeted his arrival. Dumb with terror he went into his own classroom.

Ten boys sat before him, their hands folded, their eyes bright with expectation.

'Good morning, sir,' said the one nearest him.

'Good morning,' said Paul

'Good morning, sir' said the next.

'Good morning,' said Paul.

'Good morning, sir,' said the next.

'Oh, shut up,' said Paul.

At this the boy took out a handkerchief and began to cry quietly.

'Oh, sir,' came a chorus of reproach, 'you've hurt his feelings. He's very sensitive; it's his Welsh blood, you know; it makes people very emotional. Say 'Good morning' to him, sir, or he won't be happy all day. After all, it is a good morning, isn't it, sir?'

'Silence!' shouted Paul above the uproar, and for a few moments things were quieter.

'Please, sir,' said a small voice – Paul turned and saw a grave-looking youth holding up his hand – 'please, sir, perhaps he's been smoking cigars and doesn't feel well.'

'Silence!' said Paul again.

The ten boys stopped talking and sat perfectly still staring at him. He felt himself getting hot and red under their scrutiny.

'I suppose the first thing I ought to do is to get your names clear. What is your name?' he asked, turning to the first boy.

'Tangent, sir.'

'And yours?'

'Tangent, sir,' said the next boy. Paul's heart sank.

'But you can't both be called Tangent.'

'No, sir, *I'm* Tangent. He's just trying to be funny.'

'I like that. *Me* trying to be funny! Please, sir, I'm Tangent, sir; really I am.'

'If it comes to that,' said Clutterbuck from the back of the room, 'there is only one Tangent here, and that is me. Anyone else can jolly well go to blazes.'

Paul felt desperate.

'Well, is there anyone who isn't Tangent?'

Four or five voices instantly arose.

'I'm not, sir; I'm not Tangent. I wouldn't be called Tangent, not on the end of a barge pole.'

In a few seconds the room had become divided into two parties: those who were Tangent and those who were not. Blows were already being exchanged, when the door opened and Grimes came in. There was a slight hush.

'I thought you might want this,' he said, handing Paul a walking stick. 'And if you take my advice, you'll set them something to do.'

He went out; and Paul, firmly grasping the walking-stick, faced his form.

'Listen,' he said. 'I don't care a damn what any of you are called, but if there's another word from anyone I shall keep you all in this afternoon.'

'You can't keep me in,' said Clutterbuck; 'I'm going for a walk with Captain Grimes.'

'Then I shall very nearly kill you with this stick. Meanwhile you will all write an essay on 'Self-indulgence'. There will be a prize of half a crown for the longest essay, irrespective of any possible merit.'

JAMES WILLIAMS
Life in the Raw

... the time was approaching when I was to exchange the sweet freedom of living at home for a more constrained routine. In the Summer term when I was just five, I was taken to the same local Board school that my mother had attended.

The school was situated on a hill, about 2 miles from home. Practically the whole journey to it was along footpaths, leafy lanes, over streams, through woods and fields, across churchyard with its pound for straying beasts, its gigantic haunted hollow yew, then on to the foot of the hill. I suppose there was a pinder in charge of the pound, but I never knew who he was. He was probably the sexton who lived at the Inn close by. There were only three dwellings all the way from home to the classroom. One of them was occupied by Kitty, mother's aunt, and she was a fine old dear, always good for a red apple, a sweetie, or a Welsh cake. She had a parrot which had to be removed to outer darkness when the minister called, because of his f'c'sle vocabulary. She took Hollands for her health's sake, adding sugar and hot water to the gin. My school was closed two years ago, for the policy of the Education mandarins, even in Wales where they should know better, is, to herd the children at collection points to be picked up like so many milk churns and taken in a bus to a big school in a town where they are exposed to urbanisation which is an insidious poison of the spirit. There some become smart Alecs, spivs, or what have you, but others wilt and do not develop in this alien atmosphere. The country educates, the town destroys. Smallholdings have been abandoned because they are considered too far from a bus route. The bus-borne child of today knows little of the joys of eating 'bread and cheese' off the white hawthorn, the 'bacon' from the sweet-scented briar, as succulent and tender as young asparagus, the acid astringent sorrel leaves culled from the abundance which grew in damp patches in woods and by streams, the sweet cowslip petals and the pungently sweet gorse flowers; beech-mast underneath the giant beeches in the churchyard; crab apples, black-berries, bullus, all were ours and they were free. We made our own bows and arrows, crossbows, slings and catapults. In nearly every household there was a baby, and that meant lots of elastic tubing – bought by the yard – which was used to connect the teat to the baby's milk bottle. Lengths of this elastic would be tied to a Y fork cut from the hedgerow, and secured to a piece of soft leather, usually cut from a lady's kid glove. This held the pebble or marble. Constant practice made us experts in the use of these weapons, and often we would make a woodland fire to grill our bag – starlings covered with lice but plucked and gutted, a squab, a young rabbit. Life in the raw? Maybe, but part of a sane education.

EMYR HUMPHREYS
Michael, Albie and Iorwerth

The English paper was easy, said Michael, and I wrote a lot about Long John Silver.

The Arithmetic was simple, said Albie. I finished first and walked out of the room between perplexed boys, quietly triumphant. I am able to go home early before the others come out, but I wish to wait for company in order to compare notes and answers. 'What did you get for No.6?' 'Five pounds, two shillings and four-pence three farthings?' 'That's it! That's it!', Did you get this for No.4?' I shall be among the first group going home for dinner along the broad concrete slabbed pavement, and I shall be able to tell my mother over dinner how many sums I have worked out correctly.

The Arithmetic was awful, said Michael. My mind was matted and mazed like the hair of a newly-awakened restless sleeper, like wool on thorns. My new watch thudded on my wrist like a giant pulse. It was a relief to peel the problems off my eyes, and free my limbs from the stocks, and allow my tongue to express or transmute my late discomfort, and make excuses.

We eat our lunch in an empty classroom, Iorwerth and I. The children from town walked off in a superior manner to their various homes. Some even had bicycles and we watched them wistfully as they passed the class-room window. They seemed to us the *élite*.

We were allowed to wander about the school fields and watch senior boys of the school play cricket and the senior girls play hockey. These bigger people completely ignored us, but the boys only a few years older than ourselves chased us and tried to catch us. We saw them spread one small boy on the grass and holding on to his legs and arms, bump him. 'I am determined,' I say to Iorworth, 'that they shall not do that to me.' 'So am I,' he answers. We link arms and are more friendly now than ever before, standing together watching the big boys play cricket, at last real friends, shedding unworthy thoughts.

I forgive you for being superior and copying my sums from me, thought Iorwerth.

I forgive you for being better than I at school, and for talking Welsh to me, thought Michael.

I forgive you for calling me a Methody quack-quack and a goody-goody, and for choosing Wil Ifor's company before mine.

I forgive you for looking hurt when I make fun of you, for looking pained when I swear in competition with Wil Ifor, and for making me feel uncomfortably guilty.

A party of boys came strolling up towards us, spreading out as they approached, deploying in order to surround us, camouflaging their intentions by hands-in-pockets and whistling. The leader has reached us and put his hands on my shoulder, said Michael.

'Excuse me,' he says, laughing, 'but we shall have to bump you.'

We are surrounded.

'No,' I say unsteadily, casting my eye around for an outlet.

'Oh, yes!' he says pleasantly, giving me a push on the chest so that I tumble over a boy who has knelt behind me for this purpose without my seeing him.

I am deafened by laughter and hands grasp my legs which do not even kick and grasp my arms which are like unresistant rubber.

I lie still on the grass, conscious of an ache of body and spirit and of grinning faces around me. I look around for Iorwerth. Iorwerth has gone, has fled, and, alas, I, only I, am left. I see his back making for the boys' lavatories. I think bitterly, he has deserted me and get up, brushing my clothes with my hand, walking slowly away with tears in my eyes, towards the far end of the playing fields. I turn about to survey the innumerable children bigger than I, running about the field, each with a definite place in the large red building which stands as a background to them. I am moved to tears at the thought of my own unimportance.

KENNETH GRIFFITHS
A Youthful Thespian

We infants had our own playground and it was there that I first exercised my sense of storytelling and drama. During those early years of my life, fortunately, I was allowed to go to the cinema – quite regularly. To begin with there was the Royal Gate House Cinema with its classic facade proving that it had once been a living theatre before the invention of cinematography. And I saw the original *Ben Hur*. What an impression it made on me! The handsome hero who was so hard pressed by magnificent terrifying Rome! And the villain whom I designated the Ratty Man. Where did 'Ratty' come from? And above all; the great chariot race, featuring the Hero and the Ratty Man and how the latter did such dreadful acts with his whip in the Hero's face and cutting the wheels of his chariot.

Anyway, in that infant's playground of the Tenby Council School, I organized re-enactments of the Ben Hur chariot race. I was the Hero, holding onto the shirts or pullovers of two boys in front of me. And one of these boys was Arthur Booker because he could run faster than anyone else.

I cast the Ratty Man and also supervised the other parts. Girls were allowed to be nurses. And round and round that playground we thundered. I, the Hero, surviving the pre-arranged misdemeanours of the Ratty Man. There were cut knees and the girls gave token first-aid.

Yes, I was then truly in the ascendant but I was never able to hold onto it. My mind was never with the mainstream. I was losing myself somewhere on my own and was distracting myself away from all conventional structured activities. Would I have been more 'normal' if I had had brothers or sisters. Or younger parents? I had Emily and Ernest, whom I called Gran and Gramp, and I had Lily Phillips from Pembroke Dock, who was employed to look after me. I had my very own dreams and they disallowed me from moving in the same direction as the rest. Therefore I could not compete easily; not in the classroom; not on the sportsfield; not even socially unless a few friends thought it worthwhile – and fortunately for me a few friends did. As a rule I attended chapel three times every Sunday; in the morning wedged between Gran and Gramp, in the afternoon on my own to Sunday School and again in the evening and again wedged. During the morning and evening I learnt what claustrophobia is. It was not nice. I wanted to take my clothes off; I did take my shoes and socks off surreptitiously.

In those days the services were very long, ending with the spectacular part: the sermon. And in those days there was no messing about; no namby-pamby ecumenical semi-apologizing. We were Methodists and the visiting minister would get up there and fire every gun he possessed. Some of these professional Men-of-God were famous around Wales. And they were masters of their mission. They could terrify us into appalled attention. Their varied methods in histrionics were audacious in the extreme. They came after Edmund Kean but were forerunners of Donald Wolfit, Laurence Olivier, Peter O'Toole and indeed, more relevantly, myself. There was no difference whatsoever between those preachers and the (now dying) breed of great Thespians. Both had major written works to use; the former the Bible the latter Shakespeare.

I have seen a preacher in that pulpit in Tenby build vocally and emotionally to a terrifying climax and slowly turn his back on us – we the shattered congregation. Would we take our eyes off that imperceptibly pulsating back? Would we dare!? And then round he came again, like a great feline, striking and striking directly at our apathetic failure to come to a direct understanding with Gentle Jesus during the course of the preceding week.

Of course, if there are any readers of this book who happen to be unperceptive viewers of the style of historical films which I am responsible for, I should point out that all of my films are sermons. Somehow, in me, Ben Hur had got synthesized to the Old Welsh Preachers and I am, these days, dishing out the word of history intermingled (Oh! I trust) with the Word of God. If the study of history does not consider the Great Spirit – I mean what is Right and what is Wrong – then please forget it as far as I am concerned. I only hope that my sermons on film and

thence on television are as skilful and as entertaining as my
teachers were in the old stone chapel.

MIKE JENKINS
Mouthy

Sborin', sir!
We're always doin' racism.
It's that or death, sir.
Yew're morbid
or gotta thing about the blacks.

But sir mun! Carn we do somethin' interestin'
like Aids or watch a video of *Neighbours?*
Mrs Williams Media upstairs 'ave got 'em.

Oh no! Not another poem!
They're always crap, rubbish
not enough action don' rhyme.

'Ere, sir, this one's got language in it!
It's all about sex!
Yew're bloody kinky yew are!
I'm gettin' my Mam up yer.

Sir! we 'aven' done work frages,
on'y chopsin' in groups.
We used to do real English
when we woz younger,
exercises an' fillin' in gaps.

Sir! Don' keep on askin' me
wha' we should do,
yew're the bloody teacher!

DENIS F. RATCLIFFE
Mary O'Donoghue

School was not unpleasant. Indeed, the worst thing about it was the lengthy journey to get there, through hostile streets which seemed to swarm with gangs of hostile ruffians who waged war on passers-through, especially if they were Catholics. Going home it was worse. The infants' school finished the day half an hour before the local senior school, but it took so long to walk home that there was never the chance to escape the attentions of at least two gangs on the way. In fact, mistreatment was quite mild, mostly confined to terrible threats and a fifty yard chase along the street, out of foreign territory.

Today the class spent most of the morning banging tambourines and drums, with some arithmetic in between using cardboard coins. They were left on their own quite often, and that was when the scandal of Mary O'Donoghue happened. She came to school without knickers. Not uncommon at that time, and some children came to school without shoes, even in winter. But Mary O'Donoghue was indiscreet. At seven years old she was the oldest in the class, and as Mother Superior put it, she should have known better. Mary sat down on the floor cross-legged to pound her tambourine, and soon gathered a crowd of curious boys gazing in wonderment at the complete absence of a willie. Mary battered on, unaware of the stir she had created until catastrophe struck in the form of Mother Superior.

'Mary O'Donoghue!' Heads turned at the wild anguish in Mother Superior's voice. 'Stand up at once, you sinful creature!' The boys began to disperse, sensing all was not well. 'Come here, you boys. You, you and you.' She dragged them all; about four or five of them, by the ear to a corner of the classroom. She stood over them, white-faced and shivering with rage. 'You will stay here while I send for Father Murphy,' she shouted. D., among the crowd of boys, wondered who Father Murphy was, but knew it must be serious. The pecking order was well established: teachers at the bottom, the nuns, then Mother Superior, then a priest.

'You come here with me,' she snarled to the unhappy Mary O'Donoghue as she snatched the girl's hand and hauled her out of the class and along the corridor.

That afternoon when school finished each of the boys was handed a note in a sealed envelope. None of them knew what was in it, and Miss Banbury, with an unhappy look, tucked the envelopes into the boys' pockets with firm instructions not to open the envelopes, and to hand them to their fathers.

D.'s mother opened his envelope, and read it with tightening lips. She gazed at D., who sat at the table eating cheese on toast, with loathing.

'Dirty little boy,' she whispered. 'Why did you do it?'

'Do what, Mam?'

'Look up that girl's skirt.' His mother stumbled over a more clear explanation, but this seemed to serve. D. was perplexed. He said nothing because he understood nothing of what his mother said.

'Guilty, aren't you?' she announced dramatically.

'What's that, Mam? Guilty? What's that mean?'

'Just wait till your father comes home,' she said between compressed lips. 'Just wait. You nasty little boy.'

His father read the note when he came home. His mother sat, serious, at the table, while his father ate after reading the note. He seemed annoyed. 'It's nothing,' he said shortly.

'I think it's disgusting,' said his mother. 'That a son of mine...' she paused, fashioning the theatre, '...should do such a thing.'

'It's nothing,' said his father again. 'It's not worth bothering with. Forget it.'

His mother rose. 'Well. If that's your attitude...Well!'

D. forgot it too. But the boys were never left unsupervised with the girls again. They were even separated at other lessons, the boys seated farthest away from the door, and the girls let out of the class first at break and at the end of the day.

RAYMOND WILLIAMS
Reading

As Harry rode back through the village, he passed Will on his way to school. He was in a group of children, walking together up the narrow road. There were the Jenkins children, Gwyn, Glynis, and Beth, from the cottage next to the Lippys: Howard Watkins, Will's age, from the chapel cottage; and little Cemlyn Powell, son of the widowed schoolmistress who lived next door to the Hybarts. Cemlyn was better dressed than the other children, but smaller for his age, and pale. Will walked in the middle of the group, carrying a stick. He was proud to be walking beside the leader of the group, a big boy of thirteen, who was already the size of a man. This was Elwyn Davey, from the poor family, the Daveys, whose earth-floored cottage by the Honddu had been flooded several times this past winter. Elwyn was exceptionally strong and resourceful, the acknowledged master of the school in the playground, and a match, if it came to it, for William Evans the schoolmaster himself, who simply waited resignedly for this impossible boy to leave. On Will's first day at school, Elwyn had taken him under his protection, warning the other boys off him and teaching him how to start to wrestle. Often, on the way home, he carried Will on his back, taking him down sometimes to the river, where he would wade in among the stones, with Will on his back, or sometimes, leaving Will on the sand near the acrid 'wild rhubarb' leaves, wade out himself into a deeper pool, and bend to tickle for trout. Whenever he could Elwyn took off his boots and went barefoot, though in the winters at least there was always an old pair of boots that more or less fitted him. Often he would carry Will home and put him down in the porch, breathless and laughing. Ellen did not like him, and asked Harry to tell him not to take Will off to the river. But Harry did nothing; he thought Elwyn was a fine boy.

'Hurry up, you young shavers, you'll be late,' he called as he rode past.

'Ain't shaving quite yet, Mr Price,' Elwyn shouted back, laughing.

Harry's regular term for the children was gradually being attached to Will: in school now, most of the boys called him 'Shaver'. But Elwyn always called him Will, and offered to stop the nickname if the little boy wanted it.

'No I got lots of names,' Will said to him. 'My real name's Matthew Henry. It's on my birthday paper. Honest, I saw it. Dada showed me.'

'Making out you can read,' Elwyn laughed.

'I can too. Dada showed me how before I came to school.'

'Reading,' Elwyn said, and laughed as if it were the greatest joke in the world.

'It's all right. What's wrong with it?'

Elwyn looked down at him, and put his hand, across his shoulders. 'You like what you want to, Will. Don't let them stop you.'

Will smiled, showing his missing front teeth. And we've got a book,' he said 'called *English Authors*. We read to each other out of it.'

'Aye, English,' Elwyn said. 'Only here we're Welsh.

'We talk English, Elwyn.'

'That's different.'

'How's it different?'

Elwyn hesitated, and then laughed. 'Come on, now,' he said, 'race you to the gate, give you half-way start.'

'Aye.'

CHARLOTTE WILLIAMS
Miss Thomas's Class

I graduated to Miss Thomas's class with the same cohort of neat ponytails and bobs, short back and sides and sticky-out ears. I longed for one of those ponytails that swung with the wind on sports day or a Kirby-gripped parting on the side. I longed for a pair of red shoes like Rosemary's and a vanity box and a handkerchief with embroidered edges. The girls were the natural angels and fairies, the fairy-tale princesses. They were beautiful. Diane was gossamer; her skin so delicate it was see-through. I could see the blue of her blood running through her tiny pencilled veins. She was gorgeousness all over. And Caradoc, freckles like Ma but more carefully painted on, with his hand up straight as a die to the teacher's questions. He knew everything. I was certain he would be a bank manager one day.

CARADOC JONES
Caradoc Jones
A carrot of a boy,
Sat next to me in school.
Called me chocolate biscuit
I called him ginger biscuit
Bloody fool.

Ma often came home from her topsy-turvy world shouting mad. Some *jackass* had tried to cheat her, or talked down to her, or not served her properly. And she had told them she wasn't a dog, again, and that she wasn't going to be anybody's slave. Ma spoke out with all the conceit of territory. She would fight her own people for a place for us. I had to find different ways of coping. I had to be *neis* and I hoped that nice might just mean invisible.

One day I asked Miss Thomas if I could be excused to go to the toilet. She refused. I don't know if she thought I was looking for some diversion. I can't imagine for one minute how a hundred yards no-coat walk in the rain to some cold outside toilet could have been seen as such, but her answer was 'no'. The girls' toilets are no place for a pleasant diversion. The only school space out of bounds to the teachers is not a good spot to put yourself in if you are in any way vulnerable. I've heard Pakistani girls in Newport say they would rather wait to go home at lunchtime than chance their arm in these unobserved corners. I could never have waited so long. I was always dying to go to the toilet but I would stall because most of the time, there were more important things to do. By the time I gave in and thought about asking it was bursting time. Miss Thomas said, 'No, go and sit down', her face looking like she was sucking an acid drop. She was the kind of woman who couldn't do more than one thing at a time and this day she was clearly very busy counting out pencils. She usually said lots of daft things but I reckoned it best not to challenge her. It wasn't safe. Once I got into trouble for saying 'Winston Churchill did nothing for us'. I was repeating something I had heard Ma say at home but I didn't stop to think about who the 'us' Ma was referring to, might be. Miss Thomas said lots about nation and about pride and winning the war and that 'if it wasn't for him people like me might never...', on and on she went, full of gaps and pauses when she didn't know what words she wanted to use. She was looking a bit like she might start again when she refused my toilet request so I returned to my seat as Alice. 'I don't want to be anyone's prisoner', Alice had told the White Knight, or was that Katie Alice talking?

I don't know where my idea came from but it was without a doubt related to the idea of being good. I know so because I was cultivating goodness and co-operation at the time. Perhaps all prisoners believe at some point during their incarceration that compliance will win over their captors and they will be set free. Back at my desk, I awaited permission but it didn't come. I was reading one of those books about children in foreign lands, Sue is Red Indian, and Ingmar lives in Sweden or something of the kind. Well Kimu was an Eskimo boy and his icy igloo didn't melt even though he had a fire in it. I deduced that surely Kimu's igloo was melting but with such tiny drops that nobody could see them. And so the resolution to my situation came to me. Tiny drops must go unobserved, so if I could pee one drop at a time I could get away with it. It was so obvious and so wonderful a plan Alice might have thought it up herself.

I was shocked, and so were many others when a loud warm cascade faster than the Swallow Falls at Betws-y-Coed splashed over the sides of my chair and formed a huge shameful pool on the parquet floor.

'What did you do that for?' Miss Thomas asked like Mad Hatter.

'Isn't it obvious?' thought 'Alice'.

Pandemonium broke out. Diane tightly folded her arms in disapproval, a Kirby grip still dangling from her open mouth. Paul was making a big show of jumping over the pool when he lost control of himself and accidentally pushed one of the dainties into it. She cried and so did I.

Miss Thomas could only find a large pair of boy's white football shorts and some ugly black pumps for me to change into while the 'dainty' appeared to be completely restored to her beautiful self. The ugliness of it all went deep. I was struggling on the margins of femininity already and she pushed me right over the edge. Exit Alice. I knew that I was something other than a little girl like the rest of them but I didn't know quite what. When I returned to the classroom in the humiliating garb I had to stand with my bottom pressed against the radiator all morning. 'But I'm dry Miss Thomas,' I protested. She was counting the pencils back into the box.

Part Four

When I was a windy boy and a bit
And the black spit of the chapel fold

DYLAN THOMAS
from Lament

When I was a windy boy and a bit
And the black spit of the chapel fold,
(Sighed the old ram rod, dying of women),
I tiptoed shy in the gooseberry wood,
The rude owl cried like a telltale tit,
I skipped in a blush as the big girls rolled
Ninepin down on the donkey common,
And on seesaw sunday nights I wooed
Whoever I would with my wicked eyes,
The whole of the moon I could love and leave
All the green leaved little weddings' wives
In the coal black bush and let them grieve.

JULIE RAINSBURY
Following a Saintly Path

It's hard now to think back to that time when we were all on the farm. Life was happy then and I did not realise just how lucky I was until things changed. The house wasn't grand, just the normal sort of farmhouse for these parts. It lay long and low on the hillside above the Talog brook, the cowshed at one end and the living quarters for our family, at the other, as is usual. In winter the rain dripped from the overhanging thatch. The damp seeped into the stone walls and up through the beaten clay floors but it was so cosy round the fire there at night, and it was home.

Dada and Mam had to work hard. There were one hundred and twenty acres to farm with only one hired hand to help. Still, Dada always had the sixty-one pounds each year for the landlord, he made sure of that. We were not well off, but we paid our way. We were a hard-working, respectable family. I dare anyone to deny that, even now.

Poor Mam, always busy with us children and the dairy and then the whole family down with scarlet fever. I don't know how she coped. I can dimly remember her, ill herself, dragging around the house and tending us all. I recollect the discomfort and the heat of the tossed bed and the stuffiness of the room, Sarah moaning and ill in bed beside me. No doctor, mind. Mam never made a great fuss or panic about illness. To have the doctor out is dear, of course, and most people avoid it if at all possible.

Sarah was never really right again after the fever. We all gradually got better and up and about. Sarah went back to school but seemed quieter, altered. She read even more than before. The next February she was ailing again with stomach pains and coughing. Sarah just lay in bed, almost in a stupor. I watched her silently from a little chair beside the bookshelves. I stroked her damp hand. She didn't want to eat much.

'Come on, cariad,' Mam would coax. 'You'll never be strong again if you don't eat, girl.'

Sarah said the food made her choke and turned her face to the wall. It was quite true that it often made her sick. Sometimes we could persuade her with a little stewed apple on a spoon or some warmed milk from the dairy, but she was eating hardly anything at all. Mam started to get really worried. It was outside her usual experience of the ways that illness went and she didn't know what to do.

'We'll have to get the doctor, Evan,' she told my father. 'I don't know how to help her. She's beginning to be really upset every time I mention food. She's had virtually nothing for a month now. She'll never get better at this rate.'

It was the end of February, I think, in 1867 when Mam despaired and called the doctor from Llandysul. Doctor Davies was puzzled. He gave Sarah some medicine for her stomach pain, which did seem to ease. She then terrified us all with severe fits which threw her body about the bed and there were also frightening times when she seemed to be quite uncon-scious. It was obvious to all of us that she was very ill. Indeed, after several weeks she was pale and as thin as a skeleton. The doctor visited on several occasions, for Mam was beside herself with worry, but he could offer her no real explanation.

By the autumn Sarah would not take any food from Mam at all, however hard she tried to tempt her. She was a little better and quieter and had gone back to her books when she felt she had the energy.

'You'll die if you don't eat, Sarah,' I said to her one night soon afterwards in bed.

The candle flickered but Mam and Dada had not come to bed yet and Sarah was still reading. Mam was concerned and I was getting frightened myself.

'Look, lots of the saints didn't eat,' said Sarah softly, pointing to her storybooks spread out on the bed. 'Don't let them tempt me.'

Her eyes looked rather wild and I thought she must still be suffering the effects of her illness.

'That's all right,' I said comfortingly to quieten her. 'Just take a little something now and again from me. Have something, Sarah, because I love you so much and I think you're so brave.'

So it started that, to please me, she would sometimes sip a little milk from the bottle I tucked under her arm at night when no one was about. Or, when I kissed her goodnight, she would take a little bread or cheese from my mouth that I kept there for her. She did it to please me, you understand. She knew I loved her. I can honestly say she hardly ate anything at all. She was a wonder to me. I was healthy and always hungry and ready for food. She truly was a saint in my eyes to be determined enough to survive on so little. I thought my big sister was wonderful. I thought she could do anything.

E. TEGLA DAVIES
An Outbreak of Original Sin

... grannie took the great illustrated Bible from among her hidden treasures at the bottom of an old chest which was her pride and joy. Having decided that Jimmy was now old enough to keep a secret, she promised him that he could look at the pictures in the big Bible provided he didn't tell his mother or father that she had been smoking his father's tobacco while they were in chapel. Jimmy promised eagerly, and so the dual performance began; one of them smoking and giving a running commentary on the pictures, the other overcome by the marvel of it all. He was shown the picture of Elias killing prophets, and was told that Elias was a part of his name; and he made an immediate vow that when he grew up he would not work on the road like his father, as he had once intended, but that his job would be killing prophets. She showed him a picture of the Day of Judgement, with Jesus Christ sitting on a cloud smiling at a congregation of people who looked, to him, as if they had just leapt out of bed-and-had-not-begun get dressed. On the other side of the picture mobs of devils were tormenting great multitudes of people who were perfectly respectable as far as he could see; and his grandmother informed him that he would be among the number of the tormented if he told on her.

Jimmy swore a second time, his throat dry with fear that he would never tell, never. Jimmy went to bed when the family came back, and shut his eyes tight so that he would not see the devils. He was asleep when his parents came into the room.

But at about three in the morning, there was an unearthly screech from Jimmy's part of the room. His mother leapt out of bed and lit a candle. He was sitting up in bed, white as a sheet, sweating profusely and screaming his head off. His mother tried to calm him. He quietened down a little and she was able to question him. She managed to make out the words 'day of judgement' and 'devils'. His mother was frightened. She never imagined that her youngest son had ever heard that last ominous word. Grandmother's explanation was that this was an outbreak of original sin.

DANNIE ABSE
Mr Griffiths and the Ten Commandments

I was only a small boy when I broke two of the Ten Commandments. I had never heard of the Ten Commandments until Mr Griffith took our class. Our usual teacher, Miss Carey, had to leave. The headmaster came into the classroom and whispered something to Miss Carey. He left the classroom with Miss Carey. We never learnt why Miss Carey disappeared from Marlborough Road Infants School in Roath, Cardiff. Was she a Fugitive from Justice?

Our new teacher, Mr Griffith, usually took the Big Boys. It was hard to understand him because he was a Big Boys' teacher. That first day Mr Griffith came into our class he told us about God's awesome appearance on Mount Sinai.

'Yes, dead quiet it was, children, when Moses heard the enormous voice above the strange cloud on the mountain shout; "*Anoki*".'

Glyn Parr who sat in the desk in front of me shot up his hand immediately and Mr Griffith smiled, nodded, addressed Glyn Parr directly, 'Yes, boy, you wish to know what *Anoki* means?'

'Very good. I will tell you.'

'No, sir,' said Glyn. 'Please sir, can I leave the room?'

Mr Griffith closed his eyes for a long time. Glyn kept his arm raised for a long time. For some reason Mr Griffith was not pleased. Miss Carey would have released Glyn Parr at once. Not grumpy Mr Griffith. For a moment, for several moments, it was as silent in the classroom as it had been on Mount Sinai; silent as the chalked letters A, B, C, on the blackboard; as the goldfish chewing gum in the glass tank; as the tintacks that pinned our crayoned drawings to the cork panel on the wall. I stared at the back of Glyn's head wondering whether my classmate wanted to wee-wee or do big kaka.

At last Mr Griffith revived, opened his eyes and, temporarily, ignored, Glyn's strenuously raised arm. He said, '*Anoki* is Egyptian meaning *It is I*. Moses, you see, was an Egyptian. So God spoke directly to him in his own language. If Moses had been English He would have spoken to him in English; if Moses had been Welsh He would have spoken to him in Welsh. God, you see, can speak all seventy languages and, being courteous, addressed Moses in the language of his home-patch. Anyway, the Lord then pronounced the Ten Commandments. That was a long time ago, *thousands* of years ago; but if these Commandments, to this day, are not honoured, are not kept, then beware of God's wrath.'

Because Glyn Parr was, at last, irritably released from the classroom he was the only boy who did not hear Mr Griffith, terrible of countenance, utter the Ten Commandments. After he had named the ten Thou Shalt Nots, he added, 'They are of paramount importance.' Paramount importance – I liked those words.

The late September sun no longer slanted through the tall windows. It had begun to rain. The wind had blown the sun, as mother would say, all the way to Spain. The wind blew the rain against the window-glass, making patterns on it. Soon it would be time to go home, for Mr Griffith to call out, 'Class dismiss'. When it was sunny Keith Thomas and I walked together down Marlborough Road, all by ourselves; but when it rained my mother or Mrs Thomas waited outside the iron gates of the playground with an umbrella.

'Class dismiss,' said Mr Griffith.

My mother allowed Ronnie Moore to shelter under her umbrella beside Keith and me, though Ronnie was not our friend. He was a cissy who wore knickers. Because he took up so much space I was getting wet from the dripping edges of the umbrella. The almost colourless rain delicately arrived on the pavement, darkening it, and dived into the foliage of the front gardens of the Marlborough Road houses. I felt the rain on my wrist, on the back of my neck, felt it scald the skin like the brief touch of ice. This all happened when I was still new in the world, when I could still remember my first memory, not just remember the memory of it: the sound of an aggregate of small rain on the fabric of a pram's hood, the noise that now played on my mother's umbrella.

At home my mother was troubled when I told her the few

Commandments I could remember. Thou shalt not wish for your friends' toys; thou shalt not steal; thou shalt not kill. I thought she would like to know. It was of paramount importance and it had been many years since Mama had been to school, in Ystalyfera, in the Swansea Valley. 'You're Jewish,' she said. 'I don't like you having religious instruction at school. I think you'd better have a word with your Grandfather Shepherd.'

I had two grandmothers but only one grandfather. My grandmother, Doris Abse, was a free-thinker – a 'liberated woman' Mama always said. And her children, my uncles and aunts were atheists. As was my father. But the Shepherds, especially Grandpa and Grandma, were observant Jews. The Shepherds thought the Abses to be ignorant atheists who did not know the Talmud from the back of a horse; the Abses thought the Shepherds enslaved by piety and superstition. Wilfred, my eldest brother, thought Grandpa Shepherd was a religious nut and I usually agreed with Wilfred who had recently taught me which was my right hand and which was my left. Grandpa Shepherd gave you the feeling that he had known Moses personally.

'You're the third son,' he said, pointing his grey beard at me, 'so here are three pennies for you. God favours the third. The ancestor of all humans was Seth and he was the third of Adam's sons. And of all the Hebrew kings, do you know whom God made the wisest? Solomon. And he was the third Jewish king. As for Moses, he belonged to the tribe of Levis, the third of the tribes. And Moses, let me tell you, was the third child of the family.'

Afterwards, my mother and I waited for a tram to take us back to our house in Albany Road. When we alighted at the White Wall I told my mother that Grandpa had said I was lucky to be the third in the family. She said, protesting, 'I have four children, not three. You're the fourth, the baby, the afterthought. There's your sister, Huldah Rose. You're the third son, but our first-born is Huldah.'

'I think Grandpa thinks girls don't count,' I said.

My mother nodded as if I had said something very, very wise like the third King of Israel, Solomon.

RICHARD LLEWELLYN
Puzzling Over Mankind

… we stood to sing the morning hymn, and Mrs. Tom said a little prayer, asking a blessing on us all and strength of mind and will to live and learn for the benefit of mankind.

I remember well trying to think about mankind. I used to try to build up something that would look like mankind because the word Man I knew, and Kind I knew. And I thought at last, that mankind was a very tan man with a beard who was very kind and always bending over people and being good and polite.

I told that to Mrs. Tom one evening when the others had gone and I was helping her to put Tom right for the night.

'That is a good picture of Jesus, Huw,' she said.

'Is Jesus mankind, then?' I asked her, and very surprised I was.

'Well, indeed,' she said, and she was folding Tom in a blanket. 'He did suffer enough to be mankind, whatever.'

'Well, what is mankind, then, Mrs. Jenkins?' I asked her, for I was sure to have an answer because I had puzzled long enough.

'Mankind is all of us,' Mrs. Tom said, 'you and me and Tom and everybody you can think of all over the world. That is mankind, Huw.'

'Thank you, Mrs. Jenkins,' I said, 'but how is it you ask every morning for us to help mankind, then?'

'Because,' she said, 'I want you all to think not only of yourselves and your families but everybody else who is alive. We are an equal, and all of us need helping, and there is nobody to help mankind except mankind.'

'But why do we pray to God if there is only mankind to help?' I asked, because my father was always saying that God was the only help a man could put his trust in, and what Mrs. Tom was saying was new to me.

'Only God will tell you that, Huw,' she said, and she was looking at Tom. But Mrs Tom never knew I heard what she said under her breath. 'If there is a God,' she said to herself.

WYN GRIFFITH
The Jews in Bangor

The process of mind and memory which makes small the apparently great, and magnifies the small, has destroyed the Menai Bridge, the pier, and most of the town in order to preserve a sight-and-sound image of an open window above a shop. There are gilt signs on the pane, and the chanting of young voices floats strangely high above the street in an idiom new enough to be noticed. It is neither English, as known to us, nor Welsh, but the music is cousin to our own. The marks on the window make neither pattern nor words. the door leading up from the street is always closed. While we are playing and dawdling on our way home from afternoon school, shouting, scuffling and singing, the sound of these voices rises through the network of our noise.

'Hark to them! Jews they are ... call that singing?'

'What are they doing?'

'That's a synagogue up there.'

'I'd like to go in ... I want to see them sacrifice.'

'Sacrifice what?'

'Burn a hen, kill something.'

'They don't.'

'They do. Says in the Bible they do.'

'These Jews aren't in the Bible.'

'They are.'

'There's nobody from Bangor in the Bible.'

But the argument did not end without blows, which may possibly explain why it persists in memory as the sound of a tangle of voices warmed by a rush of feeling, with a sense of personal violation at each challenging of an opposing view. The word betrays the overgrowth of later years, for it was not a matter of view, but of viewing. No question here of difference of opinion. The words that came from Tomi Williams's lips were as red as his hair, and equally part of himself: my own did not lose their uniqueness, to me, by being spoken. Nor was it a matter of belonging. My words were not chattels: they were the tendrils of my being, exposed to contact with those of another boy, so that when the dispute was ended by some adult who thrust peace (or an overriding fear) into a pavement brawl, one of the boys walked home quickly, repeating to himself the words he had made his own, nursing them in the warmth of his emotion and slowly withdrawing them into the shelter of his self-confidence. The privacy of words, their personal and intimate nature, make them a prolongation of the emotional structure of a boy, and this may be the reason why malice in deed and acts of opposition are not so potent as contrary words in beginning a fight among boys.

A little later, a Jewish family came to live next door to us. We played with the children, finding in them little different in temper or habit. They spoke Welsh and played our games. But on Saturday, our day of freedom they wore clean clothes and watched us in our liberty: on Sunday they were isolated in their freedom, restrained by the surrounding silence. As children, they lost two days each week, one for each religion. On Sunday afternoon, when we were in Sunday School, we remembered that we knew a Jacob, Levi and a Rachel. Our contacts with these children culminated in one episode which remains to this day as something seen and felt in its character of drama, and after this they disappear.

There is a privet hedge between our garden and theirs, and a girl in a white dress, with fuzzy hair, is pushing her hand between the blackened stems of the privet. I am eating a large slice of bread and jam, and she calls me quietly, looking over her shoulder towards the back door of her house as if she were afraid of being observed. She is holding out an irregularly shaped piece of thin greyish biscuit, not unlike oatcake. I take it, and give her bread and jam. She crouches down with her head towards the hedge and eats it quickly, wiping her mouth carefully after she has finished. She smiles and turns away neither of us has spoken.

I walked into the kitchen, nibbling at the biscuit and finding it tasteless and uninteresting.

'What is this, mother?'

'Where did you get it?'

'Rachel gave it me.'

'It's unleavened bread.'

'From the Bible?'

'Yes, the Bible tells you about it.'

The Bible had become true and the Jews a people.

EDITH COURTNEY

Circumcision

Dora Jones lived next door. She was delicate.

Her colourless face was lost amid thick yellow curls massing to her shoulders. Everyone said they were beautiful while Dora stood, with pale lips and round expressionless eyes, remembering the agony of having them brushed and combed.

Dora usually wore white, and sucked her fingers. She was never allowed near our front gate and I was never allowed near hers. Ours was an office, so not to be played around. Hers was just a house, but her Mother couldn't stand the noise.

We met on Friday nights, just before my music-teacher arrived, and we met like fugitives.

Though it was Mother's ambition that I should be a 'lovely pianist', it was Father's ambition to seduce my music-mistress. So, while Mother was working like mad, collecting insurance, on dark Friday nights, Father shaved with the big cut-throat razor, put on a clean white starched collar – 'Where the hell's my collar stud got to?' – combed his hair, sent me out to play, and waited.

I only ever saw my music teacher once, yet she came every week for months. Mother left the one-and-threepence fee for her and she, in return, left messages for me with Father; 'Practise Rob Roy and Donna Mobile ... AND,' Father would add, 'Keep your lips buttoned.'

My lips were buttoned so tightly even the button-hook hanging beside the mantlepiece wouldn't undo them.

If I didn't tell about the lack of music lessons, Mother wouldn't know I spent Friday nights playing in the streets where 'bad men' lurked.

But there were no bad men in our play street, Christina Street. Quite often there was no one at all except Delicate Dora, Meg and me; sometimes Olive came too, whose Father worked on the trams, and a couple of stray kids no one knew.

There were a few houses with dark panes and tiny, darker forecourts, in which one could crouch and hide; there were old trees to which one could cling and there was the little shop with steamy windows where a bumpy-nosed girl laughed until she was attractive.

There was also the place that fascinated most, the synagogue.

Its windows told us nothing, its dark-painted railings were unpeeling and fat, its small square lawn was smooth and green as though God Himself came down in secret and kept it so.

The other kids laughed about it as we stood in a group on the corner of Northampton Lane, the street lamp shading the synagogue into even deeper mystery.

'Jew boys go there!' Meg was square and ginger and common, and her Mother was, so my Mother said, 'dissipated'. Meg laughed with a big square mouth; 'I heard them say once,' she laughed more, 'I'll tell yer what I 'eard ...'

Delicate Dora leaned against the wall, light as thistledown, her yellow curls like a giant wig; 'What?'

'All right!' Meg twirled, pulling chewing-gum in a long strand from her strong teeth. She looked up at the lamp and her eyes gleamed as the gum coiled back into her mouth. She crept towards us; 'C'm'ere. I'll tell yer.'

We huddled together; sniggering now, heads down, touching; 'They cut it orf!'

She twirled away again; 'They do. They cut it – oops – right orf!'

'Garn!'

She ran away, laughing, deriding; 'It's true,' she called from the darkness. 'It's in the Bible too – you ask anybody – they can't pee, no Jew boy can. He hasn't got one.'

She was lying. She had to be.

'It's true, I say,' Meg was taunting. 'Then they keep it in a bottle. They're lined up on the altar in the synagogue. It's true.'

She climbed on the synagogue wall; 'Look! You look in there, through the window. You'll see 'em, all lined up with their names on.'

She was crude, vulgar, with a dissipated Mother. We mustn't notice her.

W.G. SEBALD
The Manse

I grew up, began Austerlitz that evening in the bar of the Great Eastern Hotel, in the little country town of Bala in Wales, in the home of a Calvinist preacher and former missionary called Emyr Elias who was married to a timid-natured English woman. I have never liked looking back at the time I spent in that unhappy house, which stood in isolation on a hill just out-side the town and was much too large for two people and an only child. Several rooms on the top floor were kept shut up year in, year out. Even today I still sometime dream that one of those locked doors opens and I step through it, into a friendlier, more familiar world. Several of the rooms that were not locked were unused too. Furnished sparsely with a bed or a chest of drawers, curtains drawn even during the day, they drowsed in a twilight that soon extinguished every sense of self-awareness in me. So I can recall almost nothing of my early days in Bala except how it hurt to be suddenly called by a new name, and how dreadful it was, once my own clothes had disappeared, to have to go around dressed in the English fashion in shorts, knee-length socks which were always slipping down, a string vest like a fish-net and mouse-grey shirt, much too thin. I know that I often lay awake for hours in my narrow bed in the manse, trying to conjure up the faces of those whom I had left, I feared through my own fault, but not until I was numb with weariness and my eyelids sank in the darkness did I see my mother bending down to me just for a fleeting moment, or my father smiling as he put on his hat. Such comfort made it all the worse to wake up early in the morning and have to face the knowledge, new every day, that I was not at home now but very far away, in some kind of captivity. Only recently have I recalled how oppressed I felt, in all the time I spent with the Eliases, by the fact that they never opened a window, and perhaps that is why when I was out and about somewhere on a summer's day years later, and passed a house with all its windows thrown open, I felt an extraordinary sense of being carried away and out of myself. It was only a few days ago that, thinking over that experience of liberation, I remembered how one of the two windows of my bedroom was walled up on the inside while it remained unchanged on the outside, a circumstance which, as one is never both outside and inside a house at the same time, I did not register until I was thirteen or fourteen, although it must have been troubling me throughout my childhood in Bala. The manse was always freezing, Austerlitz continued, not just in winter, when the only fire was often in the kitchen stove and the stone floor in the hallway was frequently covered with hoar frost, but in autumn too, and well into spring and the infallibly wet summers. And just as cold reigned in the house in Bala, so did silence. The minister's wife was always busy with her housework, dusting, mopping the tiled floor, doing the laundry, polishing the brass door fittings and preparing the meagre meals which we usually ate without a word. Sometimes she merely walked round the house making sure that everything was in its proper place, from which she would never allow it to be moved. I once found her sitting on a chair in one of the half-empty rooms upstairs, with tears in her eyes and a crumpled wet handkerchief in her hand. When she saw me standing in the doorway she rose and said it was nothing, she had only caught a cold, and as she went out she ran her fingers through my hair, the one time, as far as I remember, she ever did such a thing. Meanwhile it was the minister's unalterable custom to sit in his study, which had a view of a dark corner of the garden, thinking about next Sunday's sermon. He never wrote any of these sermons down, but worked them out in his head, toiling over them for at least four days. He would always emerge from his study in the evening in a state of deep despondency, only to disappear into it again next morning. But on Sunday, when he stood up in chapel in front of his congregation and often addressed them for a full hour, he was a changed man; he spoke with a moving eloquence which I still feel I can hear, conjuring up before the eyes of his flock the Last Judgment awaiting them all, the lurid fires of purgatory, the torments of damnation and then, with the most wonderful stellar and celestial imagery, the entry of the righteous into eternal bliss. With apparent ease, as if he were making up the most appalling horrors as he went along, he always succeeded in filling the hearts of his congregation with such sentiments of remorse that at the end of the service quite a number of them went home looking white as a sheet. The minister himself, on the other hand, was in a comparatively jovial mood for the rest of Sunday.

Part Five

I should like to be lying under the foam,
Dead, but able to hear the sound of the bell

EDWARD THOMAS
The Child on the Cliffs

Mother, the root of this little yellow flower
Among the stones has the taste of quinine.
Things are strange today on the cliff. The sun shines
                                    so bright,
And the grasshopper works at his sewing-machine
So hard. Here's one on my hand, mother, look;
I lie so still. There's one on your book.

But I have something to tell more strange. So leave
Your book to the grasshopper, mother dear, –
Like a green knight in a dazzling market-place, –
And listen now. Can you hear what I hear
Far out? Now and then the foam that curls
And stretches a white arm out like a girl's.

Fishes and gulls ring no bells. There cannot be
A chapel or church between here and Devon,
With fishes or gulls ringing its bell, – hark! –
Somewhere under the sea or up in heaven.
'It's the bell, my son, out in the bay
On the buoy. It does sound sweet today.'

Sweeter I never heard, mother, no, not in all Wales.
I should like to be lying under that foam,
Dead, but able to hear the sound of the bell,
And certain that you would often come
And rest, listening happily.
I should be happy if that could be.

LEWIS GLYN COTHI
Elegy for Siôn y Glyn

One son was a treasure to me;
Dwynwen! Woe to his father that he was ever born!
Woe to him who was left, out of affection,
to grieve evermore with no son.
Because my little die is dead
my breast is sick for Siôn y Glyn.
I am forever wailing
for the lord of boyhood tales.

The lad loved a sweet apple
and a bird and white pebbles;
a bow made of a thorn branch,
a pretty flimsy wooden sword;
afraid of the pipe, afraid of the bogeyman,
he would plead with his mother for a little ball;
Singing a note to everyone from his mouth,
Singing 'oo-o' for a nut;
he would fondle and flatter,
he would get cross with me,
and make up for a bit of wood
and for dice that he loved.

Oh that Siôn, pure gentle boy,
were another Saint Lazarus.
Beuno brought back to life again
seven who had gone to heaven;
alas once again, my true heart,
that Siôn's soul is not the eighth.

Oh Mary, alas that he lies dead!
and alas for my breast that his grave is closed!
Siôn's death is implanted there
like a stab wound in my chest.
My son, my baby's playpen,

my bosom, my heart, my song,
he was my whole mind in my lifetime,
my wise poet, he was my dream;
he was my treasure, my candle,
my fair soul, my one deceit,
my chick learning my song,
my Isolde's garland, my kiss,
my strength – woe is me after him! –
my skylark, my magician,
my love, my bow, my arrow,
my beseecher, my youthfulness.

Siôn is sending to his father
a pang of longing and love.
Farewell the smile on my lips,
farewell laughter from my mouth,
farewell sweet amusement anymore,
and farewell to games with nuts,
and farewell now to the ball,
and farewell to loud singing,
and farewell, my cheery friend,
down below while I live, Siôn my son.

WILLIAM WORDSWORTH
We Are Seven

I met a little cottage girl:
    She was eight years old, she said:
Her hair was thick with many a curl
    That clustered around her head.

'Sisters and brothers, little maid
    How many may you be?'
'How many? Seven in all,' she said
    And wondering, looked at me.

'And where are they, I pray you tell?'
    She answered, 'Seven are we;
And two of us at Conway dwell
    And two are gone to sea.

Two of us in the churchyard lie,
    My sister and my brother,
And in the churchyard cottage I
    Dwell near them with my mother.'

'You say that two at Conway dwell
    And two are gone to sea.
Yet ye are seven! – I pray you tell,
    Sweet maid, how this may be?'

'Their graves are green and may be seen,'
    The little maid replied,
'Twelve steps or more from my mother's
                                    door,
    And they are side by side.

'My stockings there I sometimes knit,
    My kerchief there I hem;
And there upon the ground I sit,
    And sing a song to them.

'And often after sunset, Sir,
    When it is light and fair
I take my little porringer
    And eat my supper there.'

'How many are you then.' said I,
    'If they two are in heaven?'
Quick was the little maid's reply,
    'O master! we are seven.'

'But they are dead; those two are dead!
  Their spirits are in heaven!'
'Twas throwing words away, for still
  The little maid would have her will:
'NAY, MASTER! WE ARE SEVEN!

FRANCIS KILVERT
The Funeral Of Little Davie

Wednesday. Christmas Day 1878

Very hard frost last night. At Presteign the thermometer fell to
2 degrees, showing 30 degrees of frost. At Monnington it fell to
4. Last night is said to have been the coldest night for 100 years.
The windows of the house and Church were so thick with frost
rime that we could not see out. We could not look through the
Church windows all day. Snow lay on the ground and the day
was dark and gloomy with a murky sky. A fair morning congregation considering the weather. By Miss Newton's special
desire Dora and I went to the Cottage to eat our Christmas
dinner at 1.30 immediately after service.

Immediately after dinner I had to go back to the church for
the funeral of little Davie of the Old Weston who died on
Monday was fixed for 2.15. The weather was dreadful, the
snow driving in blinding clouds and the walking tiresome. Yet
the funeral was only 20 minutes late. The Welcome Home, as it
chimed softly and slowly to greet the little pilgrim coming to his
rest sounded bleared and muffled through the thick snowy air.
The snow fell thickly all through the funeral service and at the
service by the grave a kind woman offered her umbrella which
a kind young fellow came and held over my head. The woman
and man were Mrs Richards and William Jackson. I asked the
poor mourners to come in and rest and warm themselves but
they would not and went into Church. The poor father, David
Davies the shepherd, was crying bitterly for the loss of his little

lamb. Owing to the funeral it was rather late before we began the afternoon service. There were very few people in Church beside the mourners. The afternoon was very dark. I was obliged to move close to the great south window to read the lessons and could hardly see even then. I preached from Luke ii.7. 'There was no room for them in the inn,' and connected the little bed in the churchyard in which we had laid Davie to rest with the manger cradle at Bethlehem.

HENRY MORTON STANLEY
Undeserved Cruelty

... in 1847, the destitute aged and the orphans, the vagabonds and the idiots, are gathered into these institutions, and located in their respective wards according to age and sex. In that of St. Asaph the four wards meet in an octagonal central house, which contains the offices of the institution, and is the residence of the governor and matron.

It took me some time to learn the unimportance of tears in a workhouse. Hitherto tears had brought me relief in one shape or all other, but from this time forth they availed nothing. James Francis, the one-handed schoolmaster into whose stern grasp Dick Price had resigned me, was little disposed to soften the blow dealt my sensibilities by treachery. Although forty-five years have passed since that dreadful evening, my resentment has not a whit abated. Dick's guile was well meant, no doubt, but I then learned for the first time that one's professed friend can smile while preparing to deal a mortal blow, and that a man can mask evil with a show of goodness. It would have been far better for me if Dick, being stronger than I, had employed compulsion, instead of shattering my confidence and planting the first seeds of distrust in a child's heart.

Francis, soured by misfortune, brutal of temper, and callous of heart, through years of control over children, was not a man to understand the cause of my inconsolable grief. Nor did he try. Time, however, alleviated my affliction, and the lapse of uncounted days, bringing their quota of smarts and pains, I tended to harden the mind for life's great task of suffering. No Greek helot or dark slave ever underwent such discipline as the boys of St. Asaph under the heavy masterful hand of James Francis. The ready back-slap in the face, the stunning clout over the ear, the strong blow with the open palm on alternate cheeks, which knocked our senses into confusion, were so frequent that it is a marvel we ever recovered them again.

In May, 1856, a new deal table had been ordered for the school, and some heedless urchin had dented its surface by standing on it, which so provoked Francis that he fell into a furious rage, and uttered terrific threats with the air of one resolved on massacre. He seized a birch which, as yet, had not been bloodied, and, striding furiously up to the first class, he demanded to know the culprit. It was a question that most of us would have preferred to answer straight off; but we were all absolutely ignorant that any damage had been made, and probably the author of it was equally unaware of it. No one could remember to have seen anyone standing on the table, and in what other manner mere dents had been impressed in the soft deal wood was inexplicable. We all answered accordingly.

'Very well, then,' said he, 'the entire class will be flogged, and, if confession is not made, I will proceed with the second, and afterwards with the third. Unbutton.'

He commenced at the foot of the class, and there was the usual yelling, and writhing, and shedding of tears. One or two of David's oaken fibre submitted to the lacerating strokes with a silent squirm or two, and now it was fast approaching my turn; but instead of the old timidity and other symptoms of terror, I felt myself hardening for resistance. He stood before me vindictively glaring, his spectacles intensifying the gleam of his eyes.

'How is this?' he cried savagely. 'Not ready? Strip, sir, this minute; I mean to stop this abominable and bare-faced lying.'

'I did not lie, sir. I know nothing of it.'

'Silence, sir. Down with your clothes.'

'Never again,' I shouted, marvelling at my own audacity.

The word had scarcely escaped me ere I found myself swung upward into the air by the collar of my jacket, and flung into a nerveless heap on the bench. Then the passionate brute pummelled me in the stomach until I fell backward, gasping for breath. Again I was lifted, and dashed on the bench with a shock that almost broke my spine. What little sense was left in me after these repeated shocks made me aware that I was smitten on the cheeks, right and left, and that soon nothing would be left of me but a mass of shattered nerves and bruised muscles.

Recovering my breath, finally, from the pounding in the stomach, I aimed a vigorous kick at the cruel Master as he stooped to me, and, by chance, the booted foot smashed his glasses, and almost blinded him with their splinters. Starting backward with the excruciating pain, he contrived to tumble over a bench, and the back of his head struck the stone; but, as he was in the act of falling, I had bounded to my feet, and possessed myself of his blackthorn. Armed with this, I rushed at the prostrate form, and struck him at random over his body, until I was called to a sense of what I was doing by the stirless way he received the thrashing.

I was exceedingly puzzled what to do now. My rage had vanished, and, instead of triumph, there came a feeling that perhaps, I ought to have endured, instead of resisting. Some suggested that he had better be carried to his study, and we accordingly dragged him along the floor to the Master's private room, and I remember well how some of the infants in the fourth form commenced to howl with unreasoning terror.

After the door had been closed on him, a dead silence, comparatively, followed. My wits were engaged in unravelling a way out of this curious dilemma in which I found myself. The overthrow of the Master before the school appeared to indicate a new state of things. Having successfully resisted once, it involved a continued resistance, for one would die before submitting again. My friend Mose asked me in a whisper if I knew what was to happen. Was the Master dead? The hideous suggestion changed the whole aspect of my thoughts. My heart began to beat, as my imagination conjured up unknown conse-quences of the outrage to authority; and I was in a mood to listen to the promptings of Mose that we should abscond. I assented to his proposal, but, first, I sent a boy to find out the condition of the Master, and was relieved to find that he was bathing his face.

Mose and I instantly left the school, for ostensible purpose of washing the blood from my face; but, as a fact, we climbed over the garden-wall and dropped into Conway's field, and thence hastened through the high corn in the Bodfari direction, as though pursued by bloodhounds.

This, then, was the result of the folly and tyranny of Francis. Boys are curious creatures, innocent as angels, proud as princes, spirited as heroes, vain as peacocks, stubborn as don-keys, silly as colts, and emotional as girls. The budding reason is so young and tender that it is unable to govern such com-posite creatures. Much may be done with kindness, as much may be done with benevolent justice, but undeserved cruelty is almost sure to ruin them.

O.M. EDWARDS
The Welsh Not

The school was in Y Llan, a few miles from where I lived. It belonged to the landowner, as did almost the entire district, and his wife, a tall dignified lady, took a great interest in the educa-tion of the locality. When I first went to the school it had a schoolmistress. I was taken to the school-house; school had already begun and not a child was to be seen in Y Llan. The schoolmistress appeared, a small woman with piercing eyes, her hands held folded in front of her. She spoke a little Welsh, the common people's language, with an English accent; her lan-guage, obviously, was English, the gentlefolk's language, the language of the parson from Cardiganshire. She could smile only when speaking English. Her face was very sour because she was obliged to degrade herself by speaking Welsh; indeed, it was sourness I always saw in her countenance, except when her thin face wore a smile to meet the generous lady who paid her wages. I did not listen to her words, and I did not like her face; it brought to mind the nose of the she-fox that I saw once, close up, after dark.

'My boy,' said my mother, 'here is your new teacher. Look at her, take the peak of your cap from your mouth, she is going to teach you everything. Shake hands with her.'

She offered me her hand, with a weak smile dying on her face – 'Oh, we shall,' she said (in Welsh), 'we'll teach him everything he needs to know; we'll teach him how to behave.'

It was not to learn how to behave that I wanted, but how to make a bridge and build a chapel. A great desire came over me to go home with my mother; but it was with the schoolmistress I had to go. The school's door was opened; I heard a strange din, and I could see children packed tight together on many benches. There were two open spaces on the floor of the school, and I could see two people on their feet, one in each open space. I understood later that they were the assistant master and mistress. The schoolmistress took me to one of them, but I only recall the words 'a new boy' from what she said. I could read Welsh quite well by then, and I was put in a class of children who were beginning to read English. The reading-book was one of the SPCK's, and I still loathe those letters, on account of the cruelty I suffered while trying to read from that book. The teacher was a pleasant fellow, and he was kind to me, but after the reading-lessons he went back to his other pupils. The word soon went around that someone new, and ridiculous at that, had come to the school. Several of the cruel children had their eye on me – I knew about them all, loud-mouthed children from Y Llan most of them were, and they never amounted to much. The teacher had whispered to me not to speak a word of Welsh; but these naughty boys did all they could to make me raise my voice, and in the end they succeeded. I lost my temper and I began to speak my mind to the treacherous busybody who had contrived to torment me. As I began to speak my rich

Welsh everyone laughed, and a cord was put around my neck, with a heavy wooden block attached to it. I had no idea what it was, I had seen a similar block on a dog's neck to stop it running after sheep. Perhaps it was to prevent me from running home that the block was hung around my neck? At last it was mid-day, the time to be released. The schoolmistress came in with a cane in her hand. She asked a question, and every servile child pointed a finger at me. Something like a smile came across her face when she saw the block around my neck. She recited some long rhyme at me, not a word of which could I understand, she showed me the cane, but she did not touch me. She pulled off the block and I understood then that it was for speaking Welsh that it had been hung around my neck.

That block was around my neck hundreds of times after that. This is how it was done, – when a child was heard uttering a word of Welsh, the teacher was to be told, then the block was put around the child's neck; and it was to stay there until he heard someone else speaking Welsh, when it was passed on to the next poor child. At school's end the one who was wearing it would be caned on his hand. Each day the block, as if by its own weight, from all parts of the school, would come to end up around my neck. Today I take comfort from the fact that I never tried to seek respite from the block by passing it on to another. I knew nothing about the principle of the thing, but my nature rebelled against this damnable way of destroying the foundation of a child's character. To teach a child to spy on a smaller one who was speaking his native language, in order to pass on the punishment to him! No, the block never came off my neck and I suffered the cane daily as school drew to its close.

SIÂN JAMES
Dora's Obsession with Death

It was well after half past nine when we arrived at Nursery School but to my surprise – she usually ignored late-comers – Sheila Wright took me to one side. 'My dear, I was so sorry to hear.'

I said, 'Oh, well, everything's all right now. John's convalescing, getting better every day, he'll be back at work next month.'

'No, I mean about you.'

'What about me?'

She looked at me strangely. 'My dear,' she said, in her little-girl voice, 'aren't I supposed to know? Oh gosh, I do hope Dora hasn't been indiscreet.'

'What has she told you?'

'About your hysterectomy.'

'Dora told you that I was having a hysterectomy?'

'What she actually said was that you were having your womb out.'

'How strange. I'm not. I'm perfectly fit.'

'But you have to go into hospital?'

'No.'

'No?'

'I'm afraid she's got hospitals on the brain. I'm sorry.'

'But she was crying about it after break on Wednesday. I had to leave Mrs Brown to cope here and take her into the garden for a little chat. I was going to tell you about it then, but I missed you.'

'My mother-in-law's friend had a hysterectomy. I suppose she heard us talking about it.'

'And you're perfectly all right'

'Yes, perfectly all right.'

'I must say, you look perfectly all right. Well. I feel a proper fool. I can usually tell in a minute when they're making things up, I can usually spot it a mile off. But she was actually crying, wondering whether you'd die and so on.'

'She does a lot of that.'

'Oh dear ...Well, perhaps it's natural in a way. I mean, with your mother dying when you were on holiday; that must have been a terrific shock for you all.'

I shook my head and bit my lip. 'My mother's not dead.'

I felt almost ashamed to belong to such a healthy family.

By this time the children were rushing about noisily from one room to another, a thing never allowed, some still in their outdoor shoes. The bad boys were actually playing Batman on the stairs; I could hear Toby's unmistakable 'Bap-man!' as he flung himself about. I'd never heard such a healthy rumpus before, not even at their Christmas party.

'She described everything, even the cemetery overlooking the sea.'

'There was a cemetery overlooking the sea,' I said, as though this excused her, 'and a new grave with wreaths on it.'

'One in the shape of an open book – white roses and carnations?'

I shrugged my shoulders. I hadn't inspected them and wasn't aware that Dora had.

Sheila Wright turned to me again. 'Do you think I ought to mention it to her? Tell her I've found out that she's been telling me a pack of lies?'

'I think it would be better if I did. I don't think she realizes what she's doing.'

'I won't say anything, then.' She sounded rather disappointed.

She moved away from me and clapped her hands for silence; and I picked up Toby and made my escape.

And as I untied her, Daisy, nervous or cross at being left so long at the gate-post, made her escape, so that we had to chase her right to the bottom of the avenue. Toby was so excited when we finally caught up with her, that he swallowed a prune stone which he must have had in his mouth since breakfast, so that I had to get him out of the pushchair and turn him upside down and thump him, to the horror of two elderly ladies on their way to the shops.

He started to roar then, not because of any pain or indignity, but because I refused to give him back the prune stone, and then to cry and sob in a heart-broken way, saying he wanted to play Batman, he didn't want to come home with me – the elderly ladies turned back, nudging each other – so that I had to take him to the stationer's on the corner to buy him a Matchbox car, and since they only had the more expensive kind I didn't have enough money left to buy the fish for John's lunch, which would mean another trip to the shops later on.

It was still only ten o'clock, but I felt decidedly worn.

BRUCE CHATWIN
Benjamin

After the harvest festival, the seagulls flew inland and Jim Watkins the Rock came to work as a farm boy at The Vision.

He was a thin wiry boy with unusually strong hands and ears that stuck out under his cap, like dock-leaves. He was four-teen. He had the moustache of a fourteen-year-old, and a lot of blackheads on his nose. He was glad to get work away from home, and he had just been baptized.

Amos taught him to handle a plough. It worried Mary that the horses were so big and Jim was so very small, but he soon learned to turn at the hedgerow and draw a straight furrow down the field. Though he was very smart for his age, he was a laggard when it came to cleaning tack, and Amos called him a 'lazy runt'.

He slept in the hay-loft, on a bed of straw.

Amos said, 'I slept in the loft when I were a lad, and that's where he sleeps.'

Jim's favourite pastime was catching moles – 'oonts' as he called them in Radnor dialect (molehills are 'oontitumps') – and when the twins left, smartened up for school, he'd lean over the gate and leer, 'Ya! Ha! Slick as oonts, ain't they?'

He took the twins on scavenging expeditions.

One Saturday, they had gone to gather chestnuts in Lurkenhope Park when a whip hissed in the grey air and Miss Nancy Bickerton rode up on a black hunter. They hid behind a tree-trunk, and peered around. She rode so close they saw the mesh of her hairnet over her golden bun. Then the mist closed over the horse's haunches, and all they found was a pile of steaming dung in the withered grass.

Benjamin often wondered why Jim smelled so nasty and finally plucked up courage to say, 'Trouble with you is you stink.'

'Be not I as stinks,' said Jim, adding mysteriously, 'another!' He led the twins up the loft ladder, rummaged in the straw and took hold of a sack with something wriggling inside. He untied the string and a little pink nose popped out.

'Me ferret,' he said.

They promised to keep the ferret a secret and, at half-term, when Amos and Mary were at market, all three stole off to net a warren at Lower Brechfa. By the time they had caught three rabbits, they were far too excited to notice the black clouds roiling over the hill. The storm broke, and pelted hailstones. Soaked and shivering, the boys ran home and sat by the fireside.

'Idiots!' said Mary when she came in and saw their wet clothes. She dosed them with gruel and Dover's powders, and packed them off to bed.

Around midnight, she lit a candle and crept into the children's room. Little Rebecca was asleep with a doll on her pillow and thumb in mouth. In the bigger bed, the boys were snoring in perfect time.

'Are the youngsters fine?' Amos rolled over, as she climbed back in beside him.

'Fine,' she said. 'They're all fine.'

But in the morning Benjamin looked feverish and complained of pains in his chest.

By evening the pains were worse. Next day, he had convulsions and coughed up bits of hard, rusty-coloured mucus. Pale as a communion wafer, and with hectic spots on his cheekbones, he lay on the lumpy bed, listening only for the swish of his mother's skirt, or the tread of his twin on the stair: it was the first time the two had slept apart.

Dr Bulmer came and diagnosed pneumonia.

For two weeks Mary hardly left the bedside. She ladled

liquorice and elderberry down his throat and, at the least sign of a rally, she fed him spoonfuls of egg-custard and slips of buttered toast.

He would cry out, 'When am I going to die, Mama?'

'I'll tell you when,' she'd say. 'And it'll be a long while yet.'

'Yes, Mama,' he'd murmur, and drift off to sleep.

Sometimes, Old Sam came up and pleaded to be allowed to die instead.

Then, without warning, on December 1st, Benjamin sat up and said he was very, very hungry. By Christmas he had come back to life – though not without a change in his personality.

'Oh, we know Benjamin,' the neighbours would say. 'The one as looks so poor.' For his shoulders had slumped, his ribs stuck out like a concertina, and there were dark rings under his eyes. He fainted twice in church. He was obsessed by death.

With the warmer weather he would tour the hedgerows, picking up dead birds and animals to give them a Christian burial. He made a miniature cemetery on the far side of the cabbage patch, and marked each grave with a cross of twigs.

He preferred now not to walk beside Lewis, but one step behind; to tread in his footsteps, to breathe the air that he had breathed. On days when he was too sick for school he would lie on Lewis's half of the mattress, laying his head on the imprint left by Lewis on the pillow.

SAM ADAMS

War casualty

These late September cloud-bleared skies, this first
Autumnal chill, recall that wartime caravan
Behind the dunes, the empty beach, black rocks
At the white edge of the sea – and a mother's pain
Of loneliness with her child, its thin limbs flailing,
Like a broken toy, but never winding down.

Each day that week, between showers and tides,
I tended the rock pool, stocked its silent world
With shells and shellfish, displayed beneath its glaze
Anemones in clusters, while in the deeps
Of a distant sea, the bones of sailors,
Swaying, swaying, made what they could of love.

And, at night, swaddled in the heavy shawl,
Never lulled by the wind's gentle rocking
Of the van, senseless to the sea's ceaseless
Hush upon the shore, the rain's sudden drumming,
The child fought sleep, its cries rising and falling,
Piercing the thin walls and heedless dark.

BOBI JONES
Portrait of a Blind Boy

We expected his hands, from watching him, to catch
    Dust, like a snail; but they went flying on
Swallowing nothing. They could no less than whisper
    Their tribulation to the air: the strain
        Of his throat was seeking a voice,
Since his whole effort was to see the globe with ears.

His eyes didn't leave his head. At times they'd roll
    Like a pair of rabbits in their cage bent on finding
A gap in the wire. But the width of their patch
    Was fairly shrunken, less than generous
        To such amiable little things
Who'd done nothing to any except to not know a jaw.

From one channel's closure, another had taken its place
    To let the world trickle into the stone
In his life. Neither sight nor hearing, despite that, gave
    A refuge for knowing. But their destination was there

Before, will be there tomorrow; this,
Igniting identity, gathered him in full orchestra.

What was it? Simply zeal of fellowship, base of memory:
    While his sight slept, this could open far:
Airfield of every expectation, wild, moderate, tame,
      That he wished his senses to welcome. Out of its cell
        He'd gaze at a flick with the skin
Of his hearing, creating a colourless face with his nose.

Still, he feared that borders might crumble like ice-cream
    His hand had been holding, melt and slip away.
He fashioned a corridor around himself, and as
      He neared at arm's breadth, there was on earth a craving
        To pretend not to be
Beneath the feet whispers of every place coming and going.

Though he peered through his hearing, there were some walls
    Less shapely than others, without a wink at anyone.
Not every voice was quite tall enough
      For his stone to capture. Then, bang; and tasting
        Nothing but blood, there was sound
Swelling red through his shoulders like a bassoon.

As he rolled on, he kept his shoes close to the ground
    Lest it start to retreat. His hands might
Become proper wings if they could now evolve
      In time, before dying. Their reach was floating there
        Above the sea of their search for the noise
Of his unbeing. They walked, keeping dry, on the certainty
                        of water.

PAUL GROVES
Blind Girl in the Garden

She, aged seven, is trying
to play with my daughter, her
exact contemporary.
Ox-eye daisies gaze at the electric
blue sky. Eyebrights witness
butterflies too drunk ever
to get their pilot's licence.
Her statuesque face is subservient
to her ears. Fingers
stretch in anticipation
of futures constantly flowering
into presents. I want
to embrace her, to spit
in the dust like Christ
and anoint her with the paste,
letting in the light.
Swallows dip in flight
as if skimming milk;
our dog bounds
over the lawn, sight as keen
as a focused camera;
the visitor ponders
and labours on tentatively.
All I can think of is
the Birmingham Millais:
two girls near Winchelsea;
a clearing shower;
achingly bright colours
and a double rainbow;
a tortoiseshell on a cloak
that would never be marvelled at;
nearby, delicate flowers.

CARADOG PRITCHARD
The Asylum

At last we came to a big gate by the side of the road and the Corner Shop Motor turned through it and went along a wide gravel drive to the door of a huge building about four times as big as Salem Chapel, with stone steps on each side going up to the door.

The Asylum, I said to myself.

Davey Corner Shop's Dad came to open the motor car door for us, and Little Will Policeman's Dad stayed exactly where he was, not moving from his seat. Mam was shaking like a leaf as she got out of the car, but she didn't say anything, and the nice lady was very gentle with her.

'You come with me now,' she said, taking her by the arm. 'We'll go and see the doctor and everything will be alright.'

And I walked behind them like a pet lamb.

There was a man in a white coat waiting for us at the door when we'd gone up the stone stairs, and he was nice too and he was smiling a big, friendly smile as he welcomed us.

'Come through here and sit down while I go and fetch the nurse,' he said, and he took the nice lady and Mam and me to a place like a parlour, with lots of chairs in a single row against the wall, and a table in the middle with a flower pot on it, full of flowers; and a big window that nobody could see through on the left-hand side, and a big cupboard on the right-hand side with two doors in it. And the three of us sat down on the chairs to wait.

And we waited there for a long time, and the only thing that happened was that Mam told the nice lady that she wanted to go to the toilet. 'You come with me,' she said kindly, 'I'll show you where it is.' And out they went and left me sitting on my own.

Then this little fat man came in and went to the cupboard without taking any notice of me. And when he tried the door, it was locked, and he started to look in his pocket for the key. He tried his trouser pocket first but it wasn't there; then his waistcoat pocket then his coat pocket and then his inside pocket. But the key mustn't have been there cos he went out again without opening the cupboard door.

Dew, he looked just like Uncle Will, I said to myself. But I was imagining things, of course.

When Mam and the nice lady came back and sat down, a pretty little girl in a nurse's uniform, about the same age as me, came in and gave us a big smile. Dew, she was a pretty little thing too, with blonde hair and blue eyes and rosy cheeks, and when she smiled at us her teeth were shining white. And she had a lot of keys hanging on a piece of string in her hand. She was exactly like Little Jini Pen Cae.

'Will you come with me, please?' she said to Mam and the nice lady, taking no notice of me. And they went with her and I stayed where I was.

I was feeling really downhearted by this time. I never thought the Asylum would be a place like this, I said to myself. I was expecting to see lots of crazy people. And then suddenly I heard a scream from behind the window and then someone started laughing. I stood up and went to the window and started thinking about poor old Emyr. But I couldn't see through the window. It's just someone messing about, I said, and went back to my chair and sat down.

After a bit, who came in again but the little fat man, and he went straight to the cupboard the same as before, without looking at me. He started looking in his pockets for the key again, only this time he found it in his waistcoat pocket. And when he'd opened the cupboard, he started taking all sorts of rubbish out of it and putting it all in a pile on the floor. It was as though he was looking for something but he couldn't find it. And when he'd taken everything out of the cupboard, he put it all back really neatly and locked the door again. Then he put the key in his pocket and started to walk out of the room. But when he got to the door, he stopped and turned round to look at me. Then he walked back to me slowly and looked at me very strangely.

'Do you know – who I am?' he said.

'No, I don't,' I said.

'Jesus Christ's brother-in-law,' he said.

Dew, I got a shock. I didn't know what to do, run out through the door or laugh in his face.

'Oh really?' I said in the end.

But he didn't say anything else, he just turned on his heel and headed for the door again. And when he reached the door he turned round with a perfectly straight face and said: 'In my Father's house there are many mansions.'

And out he went.

And I just burst out laughing.

But my mouth snapped shut like a mousetrap when another man came into the room and went to the cupboard. This one was tall and thin and his eyes looked like they were sinking back into his head. He just looked at the cupboard, then turned and came over to me. 'Did you see that man who just came in?' he said.

'Yes,' I said.

'He's not a full shilling, you know.'

'Isn't he?'

'No, he's not even a threepenny bit, really.'

And then he went out, too. I got up and went back to the window and looked all over to see if I could find a hole in the white paint, so I could see through. But there wasn't one and I couldn't see anything. So I went back and sat down again and waited. And I was still chuckling about the two funny men, the short fat one and the tall thin one.

At last, the nice lady came back in, on her own, carrying something in her hand.

'Here you are,' she said. 'You'll have to take this home with you.'

And she put a little parcel, tied with string, in my hand.

'What is it?' I said.

'Your Mam's clothes. And these, too. You'll have to take these, too.'

And she put two rings in my other hand. One was Mam's wedding ring, which had worn very thin, and the other ring was the one she always wore with the wedding ring.

I couldn't speak. I just looked at the little parcel in my right hand and the two rings in my left. And I tried to think how they'd got all Mam's clothes into such a small parcel.

And then I started crying. Not crying like I used to years ago whenever I fell down and hurt myself; and not crying like I used to at some funerals either; and not crying like when Mam went home and left me in Guto's bed at Bwlch Farm ages ago.

But crying just like I was being sick.

Crying without caring who was looking at me.

Crying as though it was the end of the world.

Crying and screaming the place down, not caring who was listening.

And glad to be crying, the same way some people are glad when they're singing, and others are glad when they're laughing.

Dew, I'd never cried like that before, and I've never cried like that since, either. I'd love to be able to cry like that again, just once more.

IAIN SINCLAIR
Lydd

Mr Lydd, a neighbour from my childhood, an ex-policeman in the RAF who finished up as an enforcer in the local asylum, a place of brutal reputation. Lydd was a widower who lived rough in his own den (a hammock in the Anderson shelter), while turning the family house over to the Irish terriers that he bred. This extended and incestuous family roamed through every room, sleeping on unmade beds, shitting on rugs, fighting like tinkers, and barking day and night at anything that moved across the garden, birds or clouds. There was a rumbling in the valley, distant thunder, and the walls of our damp cave shook; but the day was still scoured and sharp, with not a wisp of white.

Remember?

The ferns growing out of the loose brickwork brought it back. Red dust on the roped parasol. The smell of green canvas cushions, sun flaps, the swing-seat at the bottom of our garden.

Remember? How I would climb into the old oak which over-hung the garage, then drop into the next garden, a bramble wilderness; through green tunnels, filching soft fruit, fat earth-tasting raspberries; sunstreaks firing the veins in pale leaves? The only guardian, a cat, nested and yawned. This was a tame inva-sion, the house belonged to a woman who was so short-sighted she couldn't tell if it was the postman or her father, a long-dead headmaster, at the door. The bushes this disciplinarian planted had spread into a wilderness. His daughter, had I asked, would have been delighted to let me pick all the fruit I wanted.

Lydd was another matter. Approach his hedge, into which he had woven strands of barbed wire, and the terriers would bark, yelp for food – or from resentment at his return. He was fre-quently absent, his hours at the asylum were unpredictable. By temperament the man was a nightworker, patrolling empty cor-ridors, listening at doors. He wasn't a drinker or chapelgoer and he never went near the RAFA club. He wasn't seen at rugby matches. So the stories of his explosive temper, his violent assaults on patients, hapless females, were rumours that crept out from behind high walls, carried by kitchen staff or handymen.

It wasn't thunder, but a bell. A bell whose dull clanging made the bricks shake.

One afternoon, tearing my sleeve, I squeezed under the wire and down onto the roof of Lydd's shelter. This bunker had, in the years since the war, been heaped with earth that had evolved into a grassy mound; a tumulus in which Lydd could incarcerate himself. The bunker was sheltered by a dying apple tree, wrapped in sticky black tape; from its withered branches hung strips of flypaper on which numerous insects hummed.

I walked on tiptoe, in expectation of mantraps, pits filled with snakes. The shelter was an ice house in which meat would be left to survive a hot summer. Flies were drawn to the place by this sweet, rotten smell; by the oven of dog shit. By the gummy-footed fellows writhing on the blue tongues that deco-rated the tree.

The dogs at the window of the house spotted me. They jumped on one another's shoulders in a frenzy of barking. They butted the glass. I had to pee. I couldn't wait. I was wriggling with it; hopping from foot to foot, between the racket of the dogs and the manic zizzing of the flies. I ran towards the house, with the vague notion of calming the beasts by demonstrating that I meant no harm, but that only provoked them to further ecstasies. I could see that some were half-starved, others lay unmoving on the late Mrs Lydd's best armchair.

My bladder was burning. I lifted my shorts and pissed deliriously into the drain. I couldn't stop. Even when I heard the footsteps and the turning of the key in the gate that guarded the narrow passage that ran down the side of the house.

'Can you hear it?'

The gardener had moved alongside me, puffing on his pipe, happy to initiate a conversation that might postpone the moment of returning to work. He had a strange way of walking, or hopping, punting himself on his rake. I was happy to indulge him, to cut off the spontaneous eruption of a misremembered childhood. I was born yesterday, when I gritted my teeth and typed that fatal sentence: *I watched them.*

'The bell?'

Of course I could hear it. They'd hear it ten miles away in Llanthony. The foundations shook. The bell was a storm prophecy. I could see moisture being drawn from the river by the vibrations as they ran through the earth. 'No,' I said. 'Can't hear a thing.'

'Good,' Lydd replied, slipping the pipe into his pocket, 'because they call that the Lunacy Bell. If you hear it, you're mad. If you admit that you hear it, they'll take you in and burn your brain. And if you say you still hear it when they come a second time, they'll open up your head, put wires inside...'

EMLYN WILLIAMS
The Death March

… we children were invited into Mr Edwards the keeper's cottage to see Kate. She had died of something called pew-monia, aged fourteen, and it was the summer morning of the funeral. My mother, her instinct infallible, had been doubtful of the rightness of this private view, but nothing could have kept me out of the little house unrecognizable with the hooded windows.

Stiff in our Sunday best, the six of us were to be ushered in one by one, out of the sun, by the hollow-eyed mother. Doffing my cap at the front door, I remembered our standing just here six months ago, gaping in at a forbiddingly empty cornucopia; its black bowels had been emitting, in a shrill frenzied refrain, 'Daisy Daisy gibby your answer do!' As I tiptoed now into the first house I had ever visited, the maniacal voice echoed in my head. There was one floor, and I found myself straight in the bedroom. In the sudden twilight I could see nothing at first, conscious only of the overpowering smell of the strange flowers everywhere, smothering pictures and ornaments; I identified them later as carnations. The coffin lay deep on the bed, handles gleaming opulently in the half-dark; it looked too large for a pitiful room shrunk smaller still in grief. In the glassy wood I could dimly see myself; face to the wall, as if disgraced, was the gramophone horn, Daisy Daisy… I stood on my toes, cap clutched tight, eyes and mouth wide with curiosity, and looked, for the first time, upon Death.

And Death was an exquisitely pale doll who might at any minute creak up to a sitting position, open her eyes, and say Mamma. But it was Kate all right, I could see the mole she had once pointed out to us; she was wearing a nightdress, like Annie's, but she will never get up, never… 'Cusan i Kate fach' said a well-meaning aunt, 'would you like to kiss her?'. I shrank back; as I had never embraced anybody, it seemed effusive to kiss a dead neighbour. But I steeled myself to put my finger-tips to the brow, just to say I had. I had never handled ice, and the feel was chilling beyond imagination; the warm flower-smells and the hot bee-buzzing village shrivelled into nothing, the world was numbed for ever. I tried to see Annie lying there, but could not. I was back in the sun. Cassie and Ifor and John stood apprehensive, but more alive than I had ever imagined anybody; gleaming, glowing, alive. 'Welsoti hi' they whispered, 'what's she like?' 'All right,' I said, and walked home, composed but more dazed than I knew. I had never heard the village so full of noises. I shall never die, I thought, as I ate my lobscouse, never.

Afternoon came. The six of us were planted firmly in the procession, and toiled up the hill in the heat: a funereal pace in truth. From Sundays I knew every inch of the road – the crenel-lated gates of the Castle, the mushroom field, the telegraph poles; only today I could not listen to them, or even laugh insanely. The Dead March. It grew hotter; as my collar soft-ened, my heart hardened, and the opium of fancy wreathed inside my head. The mourners dabbing their eyes in the cool of the carriage, they should be doing the walking, they wouldn't perspire like this, when you mourn the only water comes out of the eyes... We were passing a cart with two stupid black-faced sheep in it, like emaciated negresses in great dirty coats; they stared at the hearse. Could sheep smell a death? Except there was nothing to smell, only a wax doll.

Squeak creak cough. Cough creak squeak. 'There was a tremor in the procession as George, pale and resolute, stepped out. "Stop!" His steady blue eyes told all, as he called out mod-estly to the hearse, "Kate!" A horrified murmur, the splinter of wood...' Ifor whispered, 'Your stocking has come down.' I hopped twice, diving for my garter at the same time; the Dead March again. I saw the doll sit up in the coffin, saw her eyelids swing back, heard her say Mamma. Then she floated glass-eyed to the dusty road, waxen hands still crossed over her breast, her whiteness a dazzle against the mourners. All eyes were upon George as he turned the handle in the small of her back; as she walked to the head of the procession, a whir of wheels. Passing Groes Chapel, her father seized George's hand. 'On Sunday, you will be thanked in Westminster Abbey!'

The daydream had served its purpose, and we were defiling

at last into the hollow of Llanasa. I put on a bereaved face; I saw a girl nudge her friend. But I was pulled out of myself when the coffin was lowered, what a waste of gleaming wood, and I heard the distraught sobs of the mother; none of us should be there to gape at such suffering. But I could not be moved, they were putting into the ground not Kate, but a doll who would never, now, say Mamma.

R. GERALLT JONES
Worse Than a Nightmare

… No more walking between the hedges to school. What did 'away' mean? Was it farther than Pwllheli? Perhaps it was as far as Bangor. Math said that the name of the place was Shwsbri, but that meant nothing. It sounded a bit like strawberries, and strawberries could be found in Llaniestyn, if only in Mr. Marret's garden. Would it be possible to fish in the pond after being 'away', or to sit on the bridge, or to go to Felin Eithin shop to buy fresh bread and eat all the crust on the way home? Could I play trains in the front room? Clic-ci-clac, clic-di-clac. Oh, Mam, I don't want to go to Shwsbri. 'Dear Mam. I don't know where I'll be when you receive this letter. I have jumped off the train. I am going to India because I don't want to go to Shwsbri away to school. Yours truly…'

I fling down the *Hotspur*, stare indignantly at Criccieth station outside, and attack my meat sandwich. It must be hours and hours since I had breakfast.

At Dovey Junction, when I have more or less forgotten the end-product of the journey, and am poking around the platform happily enough, what do I see in the middle of a crowd of people at the far end of the station but a school cap. Exactly the same colour as the sparkling new cap which is safely tucked away in my own pocket. I stand stock still. Then I creep back step by step round the corner to the gents. I stand there for a minute, my heart pumping away and my breath catching in my throat. Another boy going to the same place! Who is he? He looks incredibly clever and beautiful in his cap. I peer around the corner of the gents to look at him. He is standing still in the middle of the platform, with a new, leather case by his side. And what is he doing? Reading a newspaper! The only one I have ever seen reading a newspaper is my father. And my father is old. Do boys read newspapers in Shwsbri? Dear God, what sort of place am I going to?

When the Shwsbri train comes in, I jump smartly into an empty compartment near the back. Please God, I say, don't send that boy into this compartment. But I know perfectly well that it is no good. He arrives soon enough, swaggering his way down the corridor, cap over one ear. And in he comes. After flinging his bag up on the rack overhead and settling himself in a corner, he gives me the once-over, like a farmer at the stock-market.

'I see we're going to the same place,' he says off-handedly, pointing at the corner of my new cap that's peeping stupidly out of my coat pocket.

'I goin' to Shwsbri,' I volunteer.

'Yes, old son, we're all going there on this train,' he says, 'but you and I are going to the same school.'

'Oh. Yes.' There are too many English words chasing each other across his lips for me to follow properly. I can do nothing but sit and stare stupidly at his middle. Oh, Mam, I don't want to go away to old school, where they talk funny and boys with newspapers and no damn anybody speaking Welsh. *Diawl, diawl, diawl,* I say, leaning heavily on my lonely obscenity, I don't want to go to old school.

'I s'pose you're a new boy,' he offers, after a dreadful, long pause.

'Yes.'

'Mm. Well, you ought to be wearing your cap, you know. It's an offence not to wear your cap.'

'Oh.' I grab my black and yellow cap and stick it on my head. 'Offence?'

'Offence. Crime. Breaking the rules. What's the matter, don't you understand English?'

But the question does not require an answer, and he snuggles up behind his papers and comics to chew sweets and whistle tunelessly from time to time to show that he remembers I'm here. In Welshpool, three others descend on us, everyone laughing madly, thumping backs, pumping hands, and speaking a totally incomprehensible language, with words like 'swishing' and 'brekker' and 'footer' and 'prep'. After they've had their fill of taking each other's caps and kicking each other and flinging cases back and forth, someone notices me.

'What's this, Podge, freshie?'

'Yes,' says the veteran, 'Welshie as well. Can't understand a word of English.'

'Good God.' He gets up and stands in front of me and stares into my face. I can see the blackspots on the end of his nose. By this time, everyone is listening intently. He holds his face within three inches of mine. If I was brave, I would knock his teeth down his throat. If I was like Math or the Saint. But I'm not.

'Welshie are you? Welsh? Welsh?'

'Yes,' I say sadly, 'I am from Pen Llyn.'

Everyone starts hooting with laughter, rolling around on their seats. The questioner tries again.

'Going to Priestley School are you? School? School?'

'Yes.'

He turns triumphantly to the others.

'Bloody hell, fellers, we'll have some fun with this when we get there. All it can say is yes.'

And everyone starts rolling with laughter once again. I push myself far back into my corner for the remainder of the journey, feel the damn silly wetness in my eyes, and try to think about Cannonball Kidd, about caravans, about Barmouth, about anything but about Mam and Pen Llyn this morning. Clic-di-clac, clic-di-clac. 'Remember to write a letter.' Clic-di-clac, remember to write.

When the train reaches Shwsbri station, they all forget about me soon enough, and the whole gang rushes out on to the platform, their bags flying in all directions, caps shining new in the rain, everyone talking. On the platform, standing stiff as a poker, there's an ugly woman in a feathered hat, her lips one grim line, and a thin black walking stick in her hand. As each one of them sees her, he stops dead, pulls his cap straight, hauls trousers up, tries to get everything back into line.

'Well.' She looks at them as though she suddenly smells something unpleasant.

'Isn't there anyone else with you?'

Then she sees me standing in the carriage door, cap in hand, and my tie round the back of my neck.

'Oh.' With a come-and-gone smile flashing across her white teeth. 'Here he is. Are you Jones?'

'Yes, missus. My name is Joni Jones.'

'I see. Well from now on you'll be Jones. Jones J. We don't use names like Johnnie at school do we? And nice little boys don't say missus, Jones. My name is Miss Darby. Now boys, let's be on our way. We'll all be ready for our tea, I have no doubt.'

And off she goes along the platform, her stick clicking up and down, and her bottom waddling regularly from side to side like a duck's. And everyone follows her quiet as mice and me following everyone else like Mrs Jones the Post's little terrier dog.

I don't remember much about the next two days, thank God, only an occasional minute here and there. But I know very well that it's all far worse than any nightmare I've ever had about the place before I got here. And I had plenty of those. Everyone in this Priestley looks old and very experienced and talks a mouthful of English. The teachers have never heard of Wales, I don't think, and the cabbage is tough as string and black and green like watercress, and the bed is hard as sleeping on the floor, and the headmaster teaches something called Latin in a room with iron bars across the windows.

MIKE JENKINS
He Loved Light, Freedom and Animals
(An inscription on the grave of one of the children who died in the Aberfan disaster of October 21st, 1966.)

No grave could contain him.
He will always be young
in the classroom
having an answer
like a greeting.

Buried alive –
alive he is
by the river
skimming stones down
the path of the sun.

When the tumour on the hillside
burst and the black blood
of coal drowned him,
he ran forever
with his sheepdog leaping
for sticks, tumbling together
in windblown abandon.

I gulp back tears
because of a notion of manliness.
After the October rain
the slag-heap sagged
its greedy coalowner's belly.
He drew a picture of a wren,
his favourite bird for frailty
and determination. His eyes gleamed
as gorse-flowers do now
above the village.

His scream was stopped mid-flight.
Black and blemished
with the hill's sickness
he must have been,
like a child collier
dragged out of one of Bute's mines –
a limp statistic.

There he is, climbing a tree
mimicking an ape, calling names
at classmates. Laughs springing
down the slope. My wife hears them
her ears attuned as a ewe's in lambing
and I try to foster the inscription,
away from its stubborn stone.

LESLIE NORRIS
Elegy for David Beynon

David, we must have looked comic, sitting
there at next desks; your legs stretched
half-way down the classroom, while
my feet hung a free inch above

the floor. I remember, too, down
at The Gwynne's Field, at the side
of the little Taff, dancing with
laughing fury as you caught

effortlessly at the line-out, sliding
the ball over my head direct to
the outside-half. That was Cyril
Theophilus, who died in his quiet

so long ago that only I, perhaps,
remember he'd hold the ball one-handed
on his thin stomach as he turned
to run. Even there you were careful

to miss us with your scattering
knees as you bumped through
for yet another try. Buffeted
we were, but cheered too by our

unhurt presumption in believing
we could ever have pulled you down.
I think those children, those who died
under your arms in the crushed school,

would understand that I make this
your elegy. I know the face you had,
have walked with you enough mornings
under the fallen leaves. Theirs is

the great anonymous tragedy one word
will summarise. Aberfan, I write it
for them here, knowing we've paid to it
our shabby pence, and now it can be stored

with whatever names there are where
children end their briefest pilgrimage.
I cannot find the words for you, David. These
are too long, too many; and not enough.

ROBERT MORGAN
4c Boy

He was passive, one of seven
With a subnormal gait and a confused
Brain damaged by the evils of home
And the mean cells of heredity.
His speech was slow, peculiar,
Asthmatic, his face flushed
With fear imposed by classmates
In quiet corners of playgrounds.
His bitten fingers moved
With spastic slowness, his glasses
Pressed against his eyebrows
And his fleshy ears stuck out
Like two discs of pink plasticine.
Words on paper were strange
Symbols for his dull eyes
And ripped thoughts. Painting
Was his only source of joy.
When he laboured on rich compositions
His eyes glared over hoghaired
Brush and sugar paper.
His work sparkled with colour;
Fantasies from his imagination forced
Black unending lines of tension
Around shimmering abstract shapes.
His paintings reminded me of a tropical
Garden full of rainbows and birds
Where the sun shone in lemon yellow
Over a stream flowing with tears of despair.

SHEENAGH PUGH
Paradise for the Children

This park's got everything. The flowered fan
around the pool is a landscaped garden
that shades into woods. Paths shoulder
through holly thickets to the high field
edged with trees, a green shallow bowl
with a dark rim, and from there you see all
across the terraced streets, over to Leckwith Hill.

It's a world enclosed, from tame to wild
in little: *paradise for the children,*
but it's parents who occupy the ring
of benches round the formal pool, gazing
at the bronze eternal boy in a glitter
of light, elusive in the leaping water,
his calm classical face teasing the spectator

with the hard make of youth, the unkind
perfection. The children seeking and finding
in the bushes hanker for their freedom:
given the choice, they'd leave mum at home,
but she compromises; sits out of their way
by the fountain, hearing them nearby,
glimpsing them through the gaps of light in the dark
                                                holly.

A bronze butterfly rests on the boy's wrist:
the frailest thing on earth, and the hardest.
She listens for their voices: too long
without them, she grows restive. They're younger
than they think: cocky, trusting... That man
who was watching the ducks just now, alone,
where has he gone, and did he head in their direction?

Water splashing at the boy's feet,
he stands in a splintering of whiteness,
knee-deep in rainbows... *They didn't listen*
when I told them stay together; where's that man?
The sound of falling water, the planted scheme
of colour, is meant to leave the mind calm.
How are you supposed not to worry about them?

The man strolls back, authority in his step,
admonishes someone... he's a park-keeper.
She laughs at her fears, feeling, for an instant,
paranoid and foolish... But who says you can't
be an official, and a walking threat?
Teachers, priests, lawmakers have been that.
The naked boy poses on tiptoe, his bronze smile set

in mockery of Socrates and Plato
and all men whose wishes sink below
their words. *Did the sculptor's breath shake*
as he stroked your wax; indented your backbone
with his fingers? But you have been hardened
in the fire: no one can put a wound
on you now, so unchallengeably young as you stand,

and will always stand, year after year,
while the beautiful children of men grow older
or get used and thrown away, like some
whose mothers dropped their guard for a moment...
They wheel past, screaming like gulls; veer off
out of sight, shaking a peony's ruff
into a brief red shower, echoing the water's laugh.

RHIDIAN BROOK
Divorce

One day, his mother calls.

'I've got something to tell you, Taliesin.'

It must be serious because she uses his full name. The line is very clear this time, clear enough for her to be in the next room.

'Your father and I are going to be getting a divorce,' she says. 'I'm going to marry Toni.'

It's hard to know what to say. Taliesin's father is only a few feet away.

'When?' It's irrelevant but he asks this all the same.

'Oh, that depends. Tally, I wanted you to know that I still love you, I hope you understand that.'

'Sure.'

'I'd better speak to your father. I'm coming over soon, to collect the furniture. We can talk then, darling. Lots of love.' He hands the phone to his father. Taliesin's mother does most of the talking. When Taliesin's father has finished speaking he puts the handset down and cradles the whole telephone up by his armpit. Then he hurls it at the dresser and smashes a row of plates, several saucers, mugs and a Wedgwood gravy boat. He looks magnificent as he wrenches the phone from the wall, turning and throwing it in one fluid movement. The phone lands plumb middle and knocks the plates and saucers from their pretty place of pride. The gravy boat was one of the things his mother intended to collect.

After this athletic destruction his father bends down and immediately apologizes for what he's done. He cuts a sorry figure on his knees, picking up the pieces of shattered china and porcelain. Taliesin joins him on the floor amazed at how far and wide some of the bits have flown. One of the plates has cracked neatly in three places and is repairable. All the others are smithereened beyond repair. Not all the king horses and all the king's men could put them back together again.

His father has cut himself. His father has thick fingers designed for wrapping around things, wrenching, pulling and cutting, not for the tweezer-like picking of small fragments of china from floors. Taliesin picks up the splinters managing not to cut himself. Meanwhile some blood trickles from his father's cuts into the delta of his hands. A drop stains one of the yellow plastic squares of the kitchen floor. He holds out his palms and looks at them impressed that the needle slithers have cut him this deep. He holds out his hands in supplication.

'I'm sorry about this,' he says.

Taliesin fetches some toilet paper and presses it into his father's hands. The blood comes out treacle brown in places turning the tissue the same colour. Some of the blood stains the cuff of Taliesin's shirt. Strange to think that he came from this blood and that his mother has now caused it to spill. Although his father doesn't like sympathy he lets his son hold the tissue there for a few seconds and tries a smile of reassurance, as if to say that this plate-smashing fury is just one of those things.

'Don't think that I hate your mother,' he says. 'I don't want you to think that I hate her.'

'I know,' Taliesin says, unable to fully believe him.

'This furniture business is beyond the pale. I've had it up to here with furniture,' he says. He draws his hand across his neck to indicate where he's had it up to.

'And now she wants to marry him. I suppose it'll be one less Jones in Wales if she does. You won't have the same name as her anymore,' his father says. 'You do realize that? Not even a name will connect you.'

Mrs Rapunzel, Taliesin thinks. His father has always set great store on names but Taliesin has grown used to being called things other than his name. What does it matter that his mother will have a new one? Mrs Jones, Mrs Phillips – she will still be the same person with the same hair, eyes, teeth and things. She will still be his mother.

RACHEL TREZISE
Childhood?

The word 'childhood' causes me to remember fakeness. I feel as though I have never been a child. When I was very young I swore with the knowing, mimicking voice of someone who had spent far too much time in the company of my brother's adolescent friends. When I was growing up, developing pink nipples and my legs grew a peach fuzz which would need soon to be shaved, I thought like an old man. I watched my life with tired eyes, disappearing surely, and waited for it to end with little effort to prolong it. When finally the child was turning into a girl who should have been experimenting with make-up, I was walking a city street at three in the morning.

If I had ever been a child, I was not a child for long, and suddenly when I decided I had always been a grown-up, everyone wanted to give my childhood back.

I was never asked whether I should like to take the child abuse matters to the court. I was never asked whether I should like to have Jonesy charged with abduction. Someone saw fit to answer the questions for me: after all I was still only fourteen years old, and soon to be surrounded by policewomen, police doctors, police nurses, police social workers, barristers and judges.

It began in a social centre on the outskirts of Pontypridd. That is where I would be interviewed, the interview would be recorded and played in the Courtroom to shorten my presence at the actual trial. The upholstery was peach and pink with blue and purple stripes. The floor was carpeted with soft toys. The way my mother had made me dress could have made me look like I belonged there, but obviously I didn't feel like it. Beneath a cerise adidas sweatshirt, empty nose and earholes and a plait, I wondered what the hell difference would social workers asking me if I knew what 'consent' meant, make. What is oral sex, where exactly did he touch? Where exactly did the liquid go? Did he know about my not starting my period? I tried to answer the questions with a minimal amount of speech. I answered the Jonesy questions with arrogant single words. I didn't want to be there, I didn't have to be, so all the time I stared at the video camera and my mother watched on a monitor upstairs, I wondered why the hell I was there.

Then a doctor and a nurse laid me flat, naked on a board, holding my feet together but my knees apart. They prodded me with various metal instruments and talked about my body as though it had no mind attached. 'Looks like a skin fold to me.'

'Perhaps we should check it anyway.'

'But she hasn't mentioned anal.'

'Mmm, leave it.'

They spoke to my mother before I was let out of the room with the board. She met me at the door, took a deep breath and said, 'Well, you're not a virgin, we know that much.'

When the day of my appearance at Cardiff Crown Court arrived, my mother and I were staying at Martin's house. We missed our train because I insisted on watching the whole ten minutes of Guns n' Roses' *November Rain* on MTV, when we should have already left the house. When we got there a police woman took us through the back door to the canteen. Up until then my mother had tried to calm me by repeatedly saying 'Don't worry; he'll go down.' She bought me a ham sandwich, but I had already become a vegetarian and couldn't eat anyway.

Because I was a child, I would give evidence through a video-link up, so as not to be intimidated by the accused's face. This meant I would sit in a room at the back of the court where I could only see the judge and the two lawyers. However, the jury, the accused and the public gallery could see me. My room was much the same as the one at the social centre, full of cuddly toys. A woman in a black cloak sat next to me in case I wanted water or to be sick or something. She was overweight, with big red hair.

The judge addressed me, asking if I was all right and ready. 'Yeah,' I said. He kept repeating the question and I kept, answering "Yeah", until the accused's lawyer said, 'She is saying; "Yeah" my Lord. If you were to say "Yes",' he looked at my screen, 'the Judge might understand you.' The questioning began. 'Do you remember the video you made, Rebecca?'

'Yes'

'You said during that interview that your step-father raped you, on an average of twice a week, do you remember saying that?'

'An average of twice a week for a period of three years, that's right?'

'Yes.'

'So you are telling us that this man raped you three hundred times on average?'

'Yes, if that's what it works out as.'

The judge interrupted the court to inform the lawyers that their wigs must be removed, because they can sometimes frighten child witnesses.

The lawyer working for the accused removed his wig to reveal ginger hair which made his eyes even more black and continued with his horrible line of questioning.

'You say on your video, that the first time your step-father raped you he held you and took your clothes off, do you remember that?'

'Yes.'

'Can you explain 'how' he held you and took your clothes off.'

'He held me down and took my clothes off.'

'Yes, how did he do this?'

I struggled. And then, 'It's hard to explain how someone removes your clothes. He held me down and the next thing, my knickers were off.'

'Thank you, m'Lord, that's all for now.'

I had been informed by the police that Brian Williams's Lawyer would try to intimidate me. What it all came down to was the fact that any physical evidence my step-father had left inside me had been ruined by the physical evidence Jonesy had left inside me. All the prosecution could go on, was what I said that day, or more to the point what the lawyers got me to say. The woman acting on my behalf worked only with a case file because I was not allowed to meet her; yet my step-father was able to have many long discussions with his ginger man with black eyes. The policeman who arrested my step-father at a

Workingmen's club in Pencaerau, and then interviewed him in Aberdare pronounced him guilty right away, because he would answer questions with confidence until the word 'Rebecca' was mentioned, at which he would clam up and shake. However, this policeman, like me, could only sit and watch my hell be thrown to a jury to analyse and hypothesise, as though it was a simple case of mathematics.

CHRISTINE EVANS
On Retreat

She has been, she tells me, so careful
Of her children – cautious even of care,
But keeping them free from cold
And flies and hunger, responsible
About check-ups at the dentist
And quiet hours for homework.
Always, she would keep from them
The bare boards and the shouting
Of her childhood

Rejoicing that they have inherited
So little to reproach her for, no sign
Of short sight, crooked toes or asthma.
The easy gladness of their growing
Kept the cold wind from her back.
But now the girl
Weeps until her gaze is empty
As a wave in winter, starves her body
Because humanity, she screams, is rotten

And the small son
Whose earth-brown eyes were warm
With mischief or with wondering
Begins to ask why there's no cure

For cruelty. Now she must explain
The fairness that she's taught them
Is a game; not all the monsters
Can be spelled away in talking,
And being happy
Is a visitation or an accident.
She's here to work out how
To find some focus for the fear –
That the painless childhood she has shared
                                with them
Has not cost the toughness to survive.

ROBERT MINHINNICK
The Children

Their squints and stammers disappeared,
The crooked teeth straightened somehow.
Difficult to tell if they need you now,
These fastidious young, your children,
Sipping glittering gin through their own ice.

Talk of experience, you're still the novice:
Already they have covered the world,
England, France, it's a motorway ride
In a friend's car, the music blasting
As they overtake your careful saloon.

Yet you still pretend to know these strangers,
Passing round photographs of children
They used to be, the horses ridden,
The mountains climbed. Look closer, you think,
And you will see yourself, a figure

In the background smiling at something
Out of the picture. Yet you will wonder
At your own permanence. Make supper then,
You're good at that, but already
They are waving goodbye through the frozen

Brilliance of windscreens, driving
To a life where their backs form a tight
Circle. Are you ever discussed?
There's never a silence in their intricate conversations;
And they forgot to mention, when they are coming again.

ACKNOWLEDGEMENTS

Acknowledgements are due to the following for permission to include work in this anthology:

Dannie Abse: extract from *There was a Young Man from Cardiff* (Seren, 2001), extract from *Ash on a Young Man's Sleeve* (Robson, 2002) by permission of the author; Sam Adams: 'War casualty' first published in the *New Welsh Review*, permission given by author; Ewart Alexander: extract from *Artists in Wales* ed. Meic Stephens (Gomer, 1965); Trezza Azzopardi: extract from *The Hiding Place* (Picador, 2000); Nina Bawden: extract from 'Evacuation to Paradise' in *My Country Childhood* ed. Suzy Smith (Hodder & Staughton, 2000); Glenda Beagan: extract from *The Medlar Tree* (Seren, 1992) by permission of the author; Ruth Bidgood: 'Climbing' by permission of the author; Leonora Brito: extract from 'Michael Miles has Teeth Like a Broken-down Picket Fence' in *Dat's Love* (Seren, 1995) by permission of the author; Rhidian Brook: extract from *Testimony of Taliesin Jones* (HarperCollins, 1995) © 1995 Rhidian Brook, reproduced by permission of the author c/o Rogers, Coleridge & White Ltd., 20 Powis Mews, London W11 1JN; Jeremy Brooks: extract from *Jampot Smith* (Hutchinson, 1960); Phil Carradice: extract from *Bearding the Dragon*, by permission of the author; Bruce Chatwin: extract from *On the Black Hill* (Vintage, 1998), © 1982 Bruce Chatwin; Gillian Clarke: 'Catrin' in *Collected Poems* (Carcanet, 1997); Edith Courtney: extract from *A Mouse Ran Up My Nightie* (Gomer); Tony Curtis: 'The Infants' Christmas Concert' *Letting Go* (Poetry Wales Press, 1983) by permission of the author; E. Tegla Davies: extract from *The Master of Pen Y Bryn* (Christopher Davies, 1975) by permission of Christopher Davies; John Davies: 'For a small daughter' in *The Silence in the Park* (Poetry Wales Press, 1983) by permission of the author; Clifford Dyment: extract from *The Railway Game* (Dent, 1961); O.M. Edwards: extract from *Clych Atgof* (The Bells of Memory) translated by Meic Stephens; Alice Thomas Ellis: extract from *A Welsh Childhood* (Michael Joseph, 1990) © Alice Thomas Ellis, 1990; Christine Evans: 'On Retreat' by permission of the author; Peter Finch: 'The Tattoo' from *Selected Poems* (Seren, 1987) by permission of the author; Kenneth Griffiths: extract from *Fool's Pardon: The Autobiography of Kenneth Griffiths* (Little, Brown, 1994); Wyn Griffith: extract from *Spring of Youth* (Christopher Davies, 1971) by permission of Christopher Davies Ltd; Paul Groves: 'Children Playing' from *Academe* (Seren, 1998) 'Blind Girl in the Garden' by permission of the author; Barbara Hardy: extract from *Swansea Girl* (Seren, 2004) by permission of the author; Paul Henry: 'Boys' from *The Slipped Leash* (Seren, 2002) by permission of the author; Emyr Humphreys: extract from *Flesh and Blood*

(University of Wales Press, 1999), extract from *Toy Epic* (Seren, 2003) by permission of the author; Siân James: extract from *Sky Over Wales* (Honno, 1998), extract from *Two Loves* (St Martin's Press, 1999), extracts from *Yesterday* (Collins, 1978) by permission of the author; Mike Jenkins: 'The Woods', 'Mouthy' and 'He Loved Light, Freedom and Animals' by permission of the author; Bobi Jones: 'Portrait of a Blind Boy' translated by Joseph P. Clancy, first published in *Poetry Wales*, 'The Newborn' translated by R. Gerallt Jones from *Poetry of Wales 1930-1970* (Gomer, 1974); Glyn Jones: extract from *The Valley, The City, The Village*, extract from *The Island of Apples* (University of Wales Press, 1992) permission of Meic Stephens; R. Gerallt Jones: extract from 'Worse Than a Nightmare' in the *Penguin Book of Welsh Short Stories* (Penguin, 1994) permission of Lewis Jones: *Cwmardy: The Story of a Welsh Mining Village* (Lawrence & Wishart, 1991); T.H. Jones: 'A Storm in Childhood' by permission of the Estate of T.H. Jones; Eiluned Lewis: extract from *Dew in the Grass* by permission of the Estate of Eiluned Lewis; Alun Llewelyn-Williams: 'When I Was A Boy' translated by R. Gerrallt Jones from *Poetry of Wales 1930-1970* (Gomer, 1974); Richard Llewelyn: extract from *How Green was my Valley* (Michael Joseph, 1939), copyright 1939 by Richard Llewelyn; Ronnie Knox Mawer: *Land of My Fathers* (Bridge Books, Wrexham); Phil McKelliget: 'Baby Sitting' first published in *New Welsh Review*; Catherine Merriman: extract from 'Of Sons and Stars' in *Of Sons and Stars* (Honno, 1997) by permission of the author; Ray Milland: extract from *Wide-Eyed in Babylon* (Bodley Head, 1974); Robert Minhinnick: 'The Children' in *Selected Poems* (Carcanet, 1999) by permission of the author; Robert Morgan: '4c Boy', permission given by the author; Leslie Norris: 'Water', 'Elegy for David Beynon' *Collected Poems* (Seren, 1996), extract from 'A Moonlight Gallop' in *Collected Stories* (Seren, 1996) permission given Meic Stephens; Mary Davies Parnell: extract from *Block Salt & Candles* (Seren, 1993) by permission of the author; Caradog Pritchard: extract from *One Moonlit Night* by permission of Canongate Books Limited; Sheenagh Pugh: 'Paradise for the Children' in *Selected Poems* (Seren, 1990) by permission of the author; Julie Rainsbury: 'Daughter' first published in *Poetry Wales*, extract from 'My Sarah' in *Luminous and Forlorn* (Honno, 1994); Denis F. Ratcliffe: extract from *Second Chances* (Seren, 1996) by permission of the Estate of Denis Ratcliffe; Kate Roberts: extract from *Tea in the Heather* translated by Wyn Griffith (Seren, 2002) by permission of John Idris Jones; Dafydd Rowlands: 'I Will Show You Beauty' translated by R. Gerrallt Jones *Poetry of Wales 1930-1970* (Gomer, 1974); Bernice Rubens: extract from *Yesterday in the Back Lane* (Little, Brown, 1995) by permission of the publisher; Lorna Sage: extract from *Bad Blood*, reprinted by permission of HarperCollins Publishers Ltd © Lorna Sage, 2001; Frances Sackett: 'Newly Delivered Mother' in *The Hand Glass* (Seren, 1996) by permission of the author; W.G. Sebald: extract from *Austerlitz* (Hamish

Hamilton, 2001) translated by Anthea Bell. © the Estate of W.G. Sebald, 2001, translation © Anthea Bell, 2001; Iain Sinclair: extract from *Landor's Tower* (Granta, 2001); Henry Morton Stanley: extract from *Autobiography* (1902) edited by Lady Dorothy Stanley; Dylan Thomas: 'Fern Hill', extract from 'Reminiscences of Childhood', extract from 'Extraordinary Little Cough', 'Lament' by permission of David Higham Associates; R.S. Thomas: 'Farm Child' in *Collected Poems* (J.M. Dent) by permission of The Orion Publishing Group, extract from 'The Paths Gone By', first published in *Y Llwybrau Gynt 2* (Gomer); Rachel Trezise: extract from *In and Out of the Goldfish Bowl* (Parthian, 2001); John Tripp: 'The Children of Tenby' in *The Province of Belief* (Christopher Davies); John Powell Ward: 'Genes' (*Selected and New Poems*, 2003) by permission of the author; Evelyn Waugh: extract from *Decline and Fall* (Penguin, 1937), © Evelyn Waugh, 1928; Charlotte Williams: extract from *Sugar and Slate* (Planet, 2002) by permission of the author; Emlyn Williams: extract from *George* (Hamish Hamilton, 1960); Hilary Llewellyn-Williams: 'When my baby looks at trees' from *Hummadruz* (Seren, 2001) by permission of the author; James Williams: extracts from *Give Me Yesterday* (Gomer, 1975); Kyffin Williams: extract from *Across the Straits* (Gomer, 1973); Raymond Williams: extract from *Border Country* by permission of the estate of Raymond Williams.

About the Editor

Dewi Roberts has specialised in anthologies with Welsh themes and to date fifteen titles of this genre have appeared. He is also the author of two published books and is currently working on a volume of essays. He is active as a literary journalist and reviewer and, apart from literature, his other interests include local history and walking.

Other anthologies from Seren

Birdsong edited by Dewi Roberts £7.95

From the epic mythologies of the Mabinogion through to the present day, birds have exerted a powerful influence on the literature of Wales. This unique anthology brings together a remarkable range of poetry and prose, illustrating the varied and multi-layered responses of writers across the centuries. Fragile, yet marvellously enduring, birds are the spark for powerful writing, a cause of wonder, reverence and joyous celebration. Includes RS Thomas, Gerard Manley Hopkins, Gillian Clarke, Gwyneth Lewis, Dafydd ap Gwilym, William Condry and many more.

Christmas in Wales edited by Dewi Roberts £6.95

Celebrate Christmas the Welsh way, in the company of some of the country's leading writers, past and present. Among the many subjects drawn from stories, poems, diaries and letters are Christmas Mass, the Nativity Play, plum pudding and turkey, folk customs such as the Mari Lwyd, shopping, presents, frost and snow, and the post-Christmas blues. *Christmas in Wales* is the perfect literary companion to the festive season, a present that will be opened again and again...

A Clwyd Anthology edited by Dewi Roberts £6.95

The diversity of this north-east corner of Wales has been an unfailing source of inspiration to natives and visitors over the centuries. This collection marks the ebb and flow of history, as agriculture has declined, coal and steel have come and gone, tourism is the latest growth industry and old county towns have been eclipsed by burgeoning Wrexham and Rhyl. Among the writers are Daniel Defoe, Dr Johnson, Gerard Manley Hopkins, Beatrix Potter, Emyr Humphreys, Jan Morris, Emlyn Williams and Ellis Peters.

Love from Wales edited by Tony Curtis & Siân James £6.95

The passionate nature of the Welsh finds full expression in *Love From Wales*, a selection of poetry and prose on the theme of love in a Celtic climate. Poet Tony Curtis and novelist Siân James have chosen from the works of Wales' most intense and romantic writers in an anthology ranging from the eleventh century to the present, including translations from the original Welsh. Writers include Jean Earle, David Lloyd George, Dafydd ap Gwilym, Richard Llewellyn, Edward Thomas, Jean Rhys, Emyr Humphreys, Alexander Cordell and many more.

www.seren-books.com